children's
ministry

W9-BKD-063

VOLUNTEERS
THAT STICK

jim wideman

Group
Loveland, Colorado

www.grouppublishing.com

Group resources actually work!

This Group resource incorporates our R.E.A.L. approach to ministry. It reinforces a growing friendship with Jesus, encourages long-term learning, and results in life transformation, because it's

Relational
Learner-to-learner interaction enhances learning and builds Christian friendships.

Experiential
What learners experience through discussion and action sticks with them up to 9 times longer than what they simply hear or read.

Applicable
The aim of Christian education is to equip learners to be both hearers and doers of God's Word.

Learner-based
Learners understand and retain more when the learning process takes into consideration how they learn best.

Visit our Web site: www.group.com

Credits
Author: Jim Wideman
Editor: Amy Nappa
Creative Development Editor: Mikal Keefer
Chief Creative Officer: Joani Schultz
Copy Editor: Ann Jahns
Book Design and Production: Andrea Boven Nelson
Art Director: Helen H. Harrison
Cover Art Director/Designer: Bambi Eitel
Cover Photographer: Rodney Stewart
Production Manager: Peggy Naylor

Unless otherwise noted, Scripture taken from the HOLY BIBLE, NEW INTERNATIONAL VERSION®. Copyright © 1973, 1978, 1984 by International Bible Society. Used by permission of Zondervan Publishing House. All rights reserved.

Library of Congress Cataloging-in-Publication Data
Wideman, Jim, 1955–
Children's ministry volunteers that stick / by Jim Wideman. -- 1st American pbk. ed.
    p. cm.
ISBN 0-7644-2673-5 (pbk. : alk. paper)
1. Church work with children. 2. Lay ministry--Recruiting.   I. Title.
BV639.C4W523 2004
259' .22--dc22   2004004398
10 9 8 7 6 5 4 3   13 12 11 10 09 08
Printed in the United States of America.

How could I write a book about volunteers that stick without dedicating it to the wonderful volunteers who have served God and served me so faithfully down through the years? This book could and would not be possible without the wonderful men and women who have obeyed the call to make a difference in the lives of children at the four churches where I have had the privilege of leading: Southside Assembly of God in Jackson, Mississippi; Cathedral of the Cross, Birmingham, Alabama; Evangel Temple, Montgomery, Alabama; and to the greatest bunch of workers on the face of the earth—the people of Church On The Move in Tulsa, Oklahoma.

I'd especially like to say a big thank you to the members of our children's ministry team who shared their testimonies and stories. Thanks for being Volunteers That Stick! I couldn't lead if you didn't follow.

I also want to dedicate this book to two other special groups of people who mean the world to me.

First, the four wonderful pastors Jesus placed in my life to mold and shape me. G.D. Wilson, who gave me a chance and taught me how to work; Dan Ronsisvalle, who taught me how to dream big; Cortz Fraizer, who taught me how to believe in and love people; and to my mentor, hero, pastor, and friend, Willie George, who has taught me how to be a leader and see a vision fulfilled. Thanks for all you've done for my family and me. It's a pleasure to serve you!

Second, I'd also like to dedicate this book to my staff here at Church On The Move, past and present: Valerie Munch, Ron

Coleman, Harold Davis, Lauren Munch, Janet Harris, Lisa Munch, Bill Downes, Catherine Booker, Rachel Boucher, Sandy Lawson, plus all the interns and apprentices. You are the best.

Finally, I want to thank the folks at Group: Thom and Joani, Keith Johnson, Amy Nappa, Jan Kershner, Chris Yount, Rachel Nye, the nice girl I order books from who's always glad to take my call, and especially Mikal Keefer, for helping to make this dream come true. Y'all rock!

table of contents

Introduction   7

1   9
Creating a "Volunteers Welcome" Culture

Create a culture where volunteers are welcome, have fun, get
their needs met, and want to hang out. That's when volunteers
will stick—and grow in their desire to serve and lead.

2   25
What Do You Believe About Volunteers?

There are four things you must passionately believe before
your volunteers will ever become leaders in your ministry.

3   37
Volunteer Careers

To keep volunteers long term you've got to give them more
than just jobs—they need careers that involve significant
ministry. Here's how to make that happen.

4   57
Right People, Right Places, Right Time, Right Reasons

Want volunteers to stick? Then make sure they're the right
people in the right jobs at the right times for the right reasons.

5

Recruiting Like Jesus Recruited   68

You can't get volunteers to stick with your program until you get volunteers in the first place. Here's how Jesus got people— you can use the same techniques and get all the great people you need.

6

Job Descriptions   86

Volunteers can't be successful if they're not sure what to do. Here's how to write job descriptions for your volunteers— and why it's worth the effort.

7

Interviewing and Placement   100

Here's how to make sure volunteers get into the right jobs— jobs where they'll fit and they're likely to stick long term.

8

Orientation, Training, and Evaluation   114

Volunteers who do their jobs well tend to be happier—and stick longer. Here are three things you can do to help them be spectacularly successful.

9

The Secret of Volunteers Who Stick   128

The secret revealed...and you'll never guess what it is.

10

Photocopiable Resources   131

Here are forms you can photocopy or adapt to your needs, handouts for your leaders, and outlines and templates for job descriptions, volunteer handouts, and more.

introduction

I think of them as "Velcro volunteers."

They're the volunteers who offer to help out in children's church, and they just *stick*. Instead of helping for six months, they stay two years...five years...ten years...or more. I've got some volunteers who have been with the church for more than *sixteen years*.

Even after their own kids graduated to youth group, they're still plugging away in children's ministry, giving us the benefit of their experience. They get better and better at working with kids.

They're the volunteers I usually end up promoting because they're serving with dedication, passion, and creativity. They become leaders who direct other volunteers.

Velcro volunteers help out at VBS registration, and pretty soon they're staffing the Sunday morning registration booth. A year later they're *running* the registration booth and great things are happening.

I want volunteers like that. Don't you?

Now, at my church we've got plenty of volunteer positions that don't require someone with years of experience. I have hundreds of volunteers who give me six months or a year and then move on. That's a fact of life, and I value those volunteers, too. God bless them.

But there are positions where experience matters, and that's where I want people who'll stick through thick and thin. Who'll hang in there through times of transition, reorganization, and growth.

I'm always on the lookout for Velcro volunteers, and here's the good news: You can set up your program so you have more and more of them working with you. I'll show you how to find, hang on to, and celebrate those great people.

And I'll show you how to move them along from being responsible for small things to being responsible for big things. There's no reason volunteers can't direct and manage significant parts of your program. That frees you up to do ministry only you can do, and it makes good use of your volunteers' gifts and abilities.

With very few exceptions, Velcro volunteers are made—not born. That's a good thing for you, because by using what you learn in this book you can create the greatest volunteer staff your church has ever known.

Ready to get started?

Let's go.

chapter 1

Creating a "Volunteers Welcome" Culture

Create a culture where volunteers are welcome, have fun, get their needs met, and want to hang out. That's when volunteers will stick—and grow in their desire to serve and lead.

If you want volunteers to stick around, you've got to create a culture where people like to hang out. Makes sense, doesn't it?

And if there's one place on Earth people love sticking around, it's got to be Walt Disney World. If you've ever been there around closing time, you know what I'm talking about. Parents walk toward the parking lot *dragging* their kids behind them. The kids just don't want to leave…and often the parents don't want to leave, either.

My church surprised my family with a trip to Disney World one time, and I'll admit that even I was sorry to leave ol' Walt's world.

But why? For the average family, a trip to Disney World costs a fortune. It's usually crowded. The lines are long. The weather can be hot. And those barbecued turkey legs are good, but they aren't worth what Snow White's assistants charge at the food carts.

So what's the appeal? Pixie dust?

Nope—it's because no matter what you think of the Disney Company, they're the masters of creating environments where it's fun to hang out. I'm not sure anybody does it better than those folks.

Let's see what we can learn from Mickey and his friends.

First Impressions Count

Here's what I know with my head: To get into Disney World you wait in line. You have to buy tickets. *Expensive* tickets, too. Plus these days security people poke around in your fanny pack to see if you've got anything dangerous tucked in between the disposable camera and the peanut butter sandwiches.

You'd think a first impression that requires me to pull out a credit card and let someone search me would leave a terrible after-taste. But here's what I know with my heart: Going to Disney World is like coming home. People in funny costumes act like you're a long-lost cousin and they've all been waiting for you. You're here! Now the party can start! Somebody strike up the band!

Listen—I know it's all a matter of hiring and training. I know those ticket-takers slump off to the employee lounge and complain about their kids and their bunions just like everyone else. But if you're a paying customer at Disney World, you'll never see workers at rest or hear a complaint. Every employee is out to make a great first impression.

And their attitude is infectious. For the most part, we paying customers forget how much it cost us to walk in the door. We forget our feet hurt. We start to have a wonderful time. What's happened is this: We've been welcomed. They've looked us in the eye, smiled, and told us they're glad we're here. And we loved it.

Being welcomed—not processed or herded—is rare. And it's got huge impact.

If you want to create a place where your volunteers look forward to hanging out, make sure they're welcomed each time they walk through the door. What would happen if when your nursery director slid through the door someone shook her hand and said, "You're here! How wonderful! Now the party can start!"

First impressions. They're worth their weight in gold.

And here's something else about Disney World: Once you're through the gates, you get to be a kid again. The place is flat-out *fun*. People like hanging out at fun places. If you want a culture that's welcoming to volunteers—*make it fun to be there.*

I want to suggest four words that sum up how to create a volunteer-friendly culture: *fun, fair, forgiving,* and *faithful.*

Fun—Make your culture *FUN* for volunteers.

Here's a radical concept: *Doing ministry with kids can be fun.*

For starters, you've got lots of kids around, and they're the most fun people I know. They've got fun wired. They're always ready to laugh and play. Plus you have the chance to tell people about Jesus. That's one of the most fun things I know. And finally, you get to work alongside other people who enjoy kids.

What's not to like? Children's ministry should be a barrel of laughs. But sometimes that's not reality in a ministry.

There are lots of reasons serving in children's ministry can be the least fun hours of a volunteer's week, and four of them are all too common. I'll describe them, but not until I tell you the good news: *A wise leader can fix all of them.*

1. Leadership sets the wrong tone.

The first reason children's ministry can be no fun is that leadership can set the wrong tone. This happens when a ministry leader gathers volunteers around and somberly announces: "Now listen up. What we're doing here is the most important thing on God's green earth. We're telling boys and girls about Jesus. Don't go messing up because God's watching. He knows if your hearts are right about this. He knows if you've been praying and preparing your lessons early. You're being held eternally responsible before God for what you say and do, so don't disappoint God...or else. Keep the kids in line and don't make mistakes."

Quite the pep talk, isn't it?

The thing is, a leader who delivers a message like that isn't far off the mark. God *does* know our hearts. He *does* hold teachers responsible for their actions and words. There's nothing wrong with that speech except this: attitude.

The tone we need to set is this: We take what we *do* seriously, but we don't take *ourselves* too seriously.

Here's the same talk delivered with what I think is a healthier attitude...

"Everybody, gather 'round. What a privilege we have today to tell boys and girls about Jesus. You've prepared your lessons, prayed for wisdom, and in a few minutes kids will arrive and something wonderful will happen: God will use you. It's a wonderful opportunity for both you and the kids, so let's thank God for all the good things that are about to happen. Let's hear some laughter and let's have fun."

See the difference? The second pep talk focuses volunteers on anticipating what God's going to do. It's not all about us—how well we've prepared, how prayed up we are, how well we do at not messing up. Are those things important? Yes, but we're not the most important part of what happens in the classroom, registration area, or bus ministry—*God* is. We're along for the ride.

When we prepare hard and pray hard and then make room for cooperating with God's purposes—there's nothing more fun than that. Volunteers want to have fun. Is the tone of your ministry a fun one? Do you and the volunteers laugh a lot?

2. There's unresolved conflict.

The second reason children's ministry is often a downer is that it's no fun volunteering in a place where there's tension and hurt feelings.

Maybe two volunteers can't get along. Or someone's nursing a grudge. Or you initiated a new policy that didn't sit right with someone. Whatever it is, deal directly with what's causing conflict and unrest.

If you don't, that stress will not only affect the volunteers directly involved but also the volunteers around them. People talk, but seldom to someone who can fix the problem. Let conflict stew long enough and even the kids will sense something is wrong.

As a ministry leader, it's your job to confront situations and resolve them. A problem between people is like a problem with plumbing: neither one usually gets better by itself.

3. Volunteers are in the wrong job.

There's nothing fun about failing or doing a job that's boring or a bad fit. And if we don't place volunteers in the right spot, that's what happens. In this book I'll tell you how our church makes sure we get volunteers into the right jobs. But here's a quick tip you can take to the bank: At my church, we don't actively recruit professional educators as Sunday school teachers.

"But Brother Jim," you're saying, "aren't they the best possible

Sunday school teachers? After all, they teach all week long!"

Exactly. That's why I don't want them on Sunday morning. They've been teaching all week, and the *last* thing they want to do is face another room full of kids. They're good at it, but they're tuckered out.

I promise professional educators I'll never ask them to serve in Sunday school if they'll give me one week in the summer to help out at vacation Bible school. That's when educators are fresh and can give you their best. The result is that I've got enthusiastic teachers on Sunday and at VBS. Everybody wins. Don't get me wrong. I have wonderful professional educators helping in my children's ministry, but those who do are the exception, not the norm.

It's no fun getting stuck in the wrong job. Don't let that happen to your folks.

4. Volunteers are saddled with too big a job.

The fourth reason volunteering in children's ministry may turn out to be no fun is that most churches don't want just teachers…they want *super* teachers.

They want teachers who can leap over tall craft projects in a single bound. Who are faster than a speeding preschooler. Who can teach, fix snacks, lead music, and do it all with a smile.

For most volunteers, that's too big of a job. Maybe they're great at delivering lessons, but they can't glue two craft sticks together. Maybe they're great at follow-up, but their idea of leading music is playing the CD and humming along.

When we give volunteers too much to do—or give them jobs they can't accomplish with excellence—we suck the fun right out of the experience. When volunteers fail, it's no fun for the volunteer, the kids, or you.

I'll tell you about how to create realistic job descriptions in Chapter 6.

FAIR—MAKE YOUR CULTURE *FAIR* FOR VOLUNTEERS.

One thing about Disney World—it's fair. Everybody stands in line. It doesn't matter if you're the president of your company or the janitor—you'll shuffle back and forth on your way to the roller coaster. With a little preplanning you can "fast pass" your way to a shorter line, but it's still a line.

When a culture is fair, that means everyone plays by the same rules. Everybody knows what to expect. There's no favoritism. Most businesses operate that way because they have to; they can be sued if they discriminate. But churches often fall short when it comes to being fair.

That's surprising, because there's nothing more fair than the kingdom of God. Jesus came and died for *everyone*. *Everyone* is a sinner. *Everyone* has to be reconciled to God the same way—through Jesus Christ. The ground is completely level at the foot of the Cross.

But in church we sometimes play favorites. We give special privileges to volunteers who think like we think or who tell us what we want to hear.

Listen—that's no good. It builds resentment and hurts your program. Play favorites and you'll lose good people.

Now that's *not* to say you should treat every volunteer the same way. Jesus didn't treat his followers all the same. All were loved, all were used, and all were called...but there was an inner circle that got extra attention. When Jesus explained a parable, he took just his disciples aside to hear the inside scoop.

This principle applies to you in your church ministry, too. You pour your life into a small circle of volunteers who pour their lives into more circles. All your volunteers get what they need, but they don't all get it straight from you.

Everyone gets trained, discipled, and evaluated—that's just fair. But you don't do it all—and that's just smart. Here are three things to put in place to make sure your church culture is fair when it comes to volunteer-welcoming.

1. Set clear guidelines and expectations.

I'll tell you how to go about establishing policies and procedures in Chapter 8, but let me say this now: Being clear about your expectations *always* pays off.

If you expect certain behaviors, say so right up front. Remind people. And if people fall short, call them on it. Make an exception if you have to, but *call* it an exception. Be fair.

2. Set standards.

Everybody knows someone who got a job because she was the boss's niece. When an unqualified person gets a job, it's not only unfair, it keeps a qualified person from landing the position.

Don't let this happen in your ministry. When you ask God to send you volunteers, don't settle for just any warm body. Set standards and hold to them. Otherwise, good, qualified people won't be drawn to your ministry, and you won't have a spot open for them if they *do* come.

3. Avoid competition.

What does it take to get promoted in your outfit? Longevity? Completing training? Does a volunteer who's been in a job for twenty years have to die to make room for someone else?

Here's the thing: When people compete, they can get mean. Competition brings out our best—and our worst. I don't think anybody will deliberately push Wanda off a cliff to move her out of the nursery supervisor spot, but someone might bad-mouth her or fail to mention something good she did that was above and beyond the call of duty.

Later on I'll encourage you to address how people get promoted in your policies and procedures. Do that—it's just fair to be open about it.

FORGIVING—MAKE YOUR CULTURE *FORGIVING* FOR VOLUNTEERS.

I'm just sorry my mama didn't make it to Disney World when I was a boy so she could learn how to be a forgiving housekeeper. Try this the next time you're at Disney World: Drop something messy on the ground and spread it around with your foot. Then stand there with your arms crossed. Inside a few minutes, a smiling, bright-eyed groundskeeper will show up with a whisk broom and clean it up. No yelling. No nasty looks. No throwing you out of the park.

Now if *I'd* done that when I was a boy, my mama would have shown up right away too—but she wouldn't have been smiling. And she wouldn't have been carrying a whisk broom.

If you want to see a lifestyle of forgiveness in action, watch the characters wandering around Disney World. Goofy will give you a hug and pose for a picture whether you're clean or dirty, tall or small, smiling or frowning. What the actors who wear the costumes talk about backstage I don't know, but when they're with the public, they'll forgive just about anything.

How forgiving and tolerant is your ministry with volunteers? How many times can someone mess up and still be welcome? Now I'm not talking about doing something terrible like abusing a child. There's no room for tolerance when it comes to that—there'll be forgiveness, but also consequences. I'm talking about everyday mistakes people tend to make.

If you want volunteers to stick, they've got to know you're forgiving. Because they already know they're likely to need forgiveness now and then.

Here are three ways to create a forgiving culture.

1. Be gracious.

Extend the same grace to others that you've received.

When you first started in children's ministry, you didn't know how to deliver a children's sermon, either. You made all the mistakes that you're watching your volunteers make. So come alongside them, put a hand on their shoulders, and train them. And be gentle as you do it.

2. Share stories about your own failures.

Some of your volunteers think that just because you're a ministry leader, you float to the breakfast table and tell the cereal, "Let there be milk," and the Rice Krispies start snapping away like crazy.

Listen—you know that's not true. So don't let your volunteers believe things like that about you. Tell them about that time you were making balloon animals and got something wrong, and you managed to make a sculpture that was *way* inappropriate. Or the time you couldn't get the curtains open on the puppet stage. Or how you managed to forget a meeting and left twenty parents sitting in a room without a leader.

Stories like that tell your team you understand messing up. And while you don't encourage mistakes, it's not the end of the world.

3. Have a sense of humor.

All wasn't lost when the bus driver accidentally backed into the senior pastor's new car, right? The church won't close down because your nursery team leader forgot to take out the dirty diapers after Wednesday night's service. So don't act like those situations are the worst thing that's ever happened.

Look at it this way: After that nursery supervisor has to take care of the mess on Sunday morning and air out the room, that's a mistake she'll *never* make again, guaranteed. Buy her an air freshener, a couple of nose plugs, and a card telling her you're glad she's on the team. Let her know you forgive her.

Be forgiving and that's what will come back to you—again and again.

FAITHFUL—MAKE YOUR CULTURE *FAITHFUL* FOR VOLUNTEERS.

A faithful culture is one where volunteers trust their leaders. It's where volunteers know leaders have the volunteers' best interests at heart. The children's pastor isn't going to burn out volunteers to get a program off the ground. Too many times volunteers have to take what they're told with a grain of salt. With a *tablespoon* of salt!

"Don't worry, there won't be more than a few kids in the nursery" turns into thirty bawling babies and too few staff.

"Little Brian is a handful, but you'll do fine" doesn't make clear that Brian is so active his parents nicknamed him "Bruiser." And he's bringing his little buddy, "Timmy the Terror," to class with him.

Can your staff trust you? Have you given them *reason* to trust you?

Here are four ways to establish a faithful environment for your volunteers.

1. Deliver what you promise.

Here's where I think Disney World falls down a little bit. Disney World calls itself "the happiest place on earth." That's one *big* claim, and for at least a few families who misplace a child for an hour or so, or who have to stand in a particularly slow line, it's not a happy place at all. It's a stressful place. It's a place they wish they'd never seen.

But you can't fault the Disney folks for trying to deliver whatever it takes to let guests have a good time.

Unfortunately, we often fail at doing whatever it takes to make sure our volunteers have a great time. We forget to follow through. We don't tell them what to expect. We overpromise or underdeliver.

Be sure you do *what* you say you'll do, *when* you say you'll do it. Do that nine times in a row and your people will forgive you when you blow it on number ten. They already know you're imperfect—you won't shock them.

2. Give credit where credit is due.

Ask yourself, "If my entire team of volunteers quit today, how would things go next Sunday?" At Church On The Move, we'd melt down in a heartbeat. If you come visit us some Sunday and you leave thinking, "That Brother Jim has things nailed down. This place is just humming along so smoothly," you've made a mistake. I'm glad you had a great experience, but you shouldn't be thanking me.

I'm not the one who showed you to a parking spot or helped you check your kids into our children's ministry program. I didn't teach the lesson. I didn't serve the snacks.

All of that happened because of excellent, well-trained volunteers who are serving out of their passion, skills, and strengths. And if you catch me in person with your compliment, I'll redirect you to those people.

Did I have something to do with getting those people in place and ready for you and your kids? I sure did...but that's backstage stuff. You thank them and I'll feel thanked enough.

3. Use your magic words.

My mama taught me that there were magic words I was supposed to use every chance I could: *please* and *thank you*. She was right. They work wonders with volunteers (and with paid staff, too).

Those words communicate "I see you." They communicate "I appreciate you." They communicate "How about you keep coming back to do what you've been doing?" So remember Mama's advice, and say the magic words—often.

4. Take your culture's temperature now and then.

Does your church have a volunteer-welcoming culture? It's good to know, because slick volunteer recruitment won't make a bit of difference if once people sign up they don't like how you do business.

Think about Disney World again. Disney spends a fortune on advertising that it's a great vacation spot. But if kids bounce through the gates and all they find is Grumpy the Dwarf and a couple of lame rides, what's going to happen?

I'll tell you: Disney will be out of business in six months. Disappointed people talk, and they talk *loudly*. It'll be all over the Web, all over the news, and for Disney it'll be all over—period.

People talk about what it's like to volunteer in your ministry too. They talk about what the leadership is like, whether it's fun to volunteer, and whether they plan on coming back. People are talking...but what are they saying?

If you want to build long-term Velcro volunteers, you've got to have a culture that encourages people to stick around. *You* may think you've accomplished that, but what do people in your church think?

Ask them. On page 20 you'll find a quick survey to give your volunteers. Before you distribute it, ask someone you trust to collect the completed forms, type up a summary, and destroy the original surveys. That way volunteers can give their honest opinions anonymously. When you see how your church's current culture is evaluated, it might be an eye-opener.

Your church's culture will make or break your volunteer program. If it's not fun, fair, forgiving, and faithful, you won't hang on to volunteers long. Fall too short of that ideal culture and not only won't you have volunteers that stick—you won't have volunteers at all.

Is your culture one that welcomes and develops volunteers? Give the survey a try. See what you learn.

volunteer
evaluation

Date: _____ Your volunteer role: _____

Name (optional) _____

Phone (optional) _____

Please rate your volunteer experience by checking one column for each question:

SD = Strongly Disagree   **D** = Disagree   **A** = Agree   **SA** = Strongly Agree

Fun: How much fun is it to volunteer at our church?

	SD	D	A	SA
1. I tell friends and family about enjoyable things that happen to me in my volunteer role at church.				
2. I laugh often when I'm volunteering.				
3. I enjoy seeing the people I've met through my volunteer role.				
4. I feel I'm in the right volunteer job.				
5. My leaders value me and tell me they value me.				
6. I have the training to do my volunteer job with excellence.				
7. I have the resources to do my volunteer job with excellence.				
8. I look forward to serving in my volunteer job.				

Fair: In your volunteer role are you treated fairly?

	SD	D	A	SA
9. The person who directs me in my volunteer role plays favorites among volunteers.				
10. The rules I'm expected to obey are clear to me.				
11. When I fail to meet a job expectation, I receive coaching to help me improve.				
12. I'm reviewed regularly and receive insight into how I'm doing in my volunteer role.				
13. As a volunteer, my opinion counts.				
14. In my volunteer role, I'm treated with respect.				

Forgiving: In your volunteer role are you expected to be perfect—or just growing?

	SD	D	A	SA
15. If I made a mistake that affected the ministry, I'd feel comfortable telling my leader about it.				
16. The person who directs me in my volunteer role doesn't talk about other volunteers' mistakes in a harsh way or behind their backs.				
17. The person who directs me in my volunteer role has shared with me something he or she did that wasn't successful.				
18. In the area in which I volunteer, we have a sense of humor about mistakes that aren't serious.				

Faithful: How much trust do you have in your leaders?

	SD	D	A	SA
19. The person who directs me in my volunteer role cares for me personally.				
20. I can talk about requests from my leader and be listened to.				
21. The person who directs me in my volunteer role keeps his or her promises.				
22. The person who directs me in my volunteer role gives me credit when I do something that's appreciated.				
23. The person who directs me in my volunteer role is the sort of person I'd trust to pay me back if he or she borrowed ten dollars.				
24. Overall, I am happy with my experience as a volunteer.				
25. If my circumstances allow it, I will continue to volunteer in the future.				
26. I believe my leader is following God's direction.				

Creating a volunteer-welcoming culture is huge, and you can't do it alone. You need to get lots of people on board, especially people in leadership. Jot down the names of people who are already making your church's volunteer culture a place that's fun, fair, forgiving, and faithful. Who's already helping? And whom do you need to recruit?

You're on the hook to help out across the board—but who else needs to be standing right there next to you? Which leaders and other people are impacting your culture now—for better or worse? Write their names below, with a quick note as to why you listed them. Let's find out who's already on your team and who needs some convincing:

Fun

_____

_____

_____

_____

_____

_____

Fair

_____

_____

_____

_____

_____

Forgiving

_____

_____

_____

_____

Faithful

Some of your people are already doing a bang-up job, aren't they? I'll tell you, there are departments at my church where volunteers laugh so hard they cry. They love getting together to work, and they love hanging out together as friends. It's just the coolest thing to watch.

But there are probably some people you listed who need a little help. Maybe they play favorites and working with them isn't fair. Or they're carrying around grudges. Or they don't do what they say they'll do. Mark my words: Those people are hurting your culture.

Consider Disney World again. They'll let you get away with a lot, but if you cross the line and start ruining the culture of the theme park, you're history. If a guest got mad and started swearing and carrying on, security *would* be called. And the guest's friends *would* be picking him up at the gate as they left. That guest would definitely *not* be joining them for dinner in Cinderella's Castle.

Disney World is a fierce defender of its culture. And it's smart for you to do the same. Don't let anyone go chasing volunteers away because of a nasty attitude or a lack of commitment to the vision of your church and ministry.

Creating a volunteer-welcoming culture is a great first step— but it's *just* a first step. It'll make volunteering at your church attractive, but it's not going to keep people on board an especially long time. For that to happen, you'll have to put some other things in place.

Here's the truth: Most of what you do to turn volunteers into long-term volunteers who stick—the Velcro volunteers I've described—you have to do anyway, just to have a healthy volunteer program.

I'll run through all the steps you need to take. I'll do that because until you've got *those* things in place, you're not ready to welcome the long-term, Velcro volunteers God's going to send your way!

chapter 2

What Do You Believe About Volunteers?

There are four things you must passionately believe before your volunteers will ever become leaders in your ministry.

I get to speak at lots of churches, and I'll tell you something: If you invite me into your church, I'll be able to tell you inside an hour what you think of volunteers. Not what you *say* about them. I already know what you'll *say* about them. You'll say they're the most important people on the planet, that you couldn't get along without them, and that you thank God every day for each of them.

But those are just words.

Listen, if I come to your church and it's obvious you've been up all night running around setting up tables and chairs, that says something. It says you don't trust your volunteers to follow through and get things right. Or it might say that you forgot to ask for help—and that says something about you and your volunteers, too.

If you're relaxed and ready to greet your guests while volunteers take care of all the details, that tells me you've delegated responsibility to others. You're using your volunteers well. And if I see a problem come up and those volunteers go to another volunteer to get the problem solved, that tells me you've delegated some authority, too. Good for you. There's nothing more frustrating for volunteers than to have responsibility and no authority, but it happens all the time.

Turning Your Volunteers Into Leaders

We're going to talk about how you can turn your volunteers into leaders, but something has to happen before that process starts: *You've got to believe the right things about volunteers.*

If there's one thing I hate hearing, it's this: "Oh, she's just a volunteer." I also hate it when people come up to tell me about what they do in ministry, point to themselves and say, "*I'm* just a volunteer."

Friend, there's no such thing as *just* a volunteer!

When people who are serving Jesus think that they're not important because they're not getting a paycheck, they're thinking wrong. They're giving the enemy a stronghold. I know your dictionary tells you that a stronghold is a fort that's used for defense, but in my way of thinking it can also be used as a camp from which the enemy can attack you.

When you believe wrong information about the kingdom of God and your place in it, it gives the enemy a stronghold. You start believing that paid staff members at church are important and unpaid people aren't. You start believing that only people with "Pastor" in front of their names can do real ministry. That's a stronghold, and we've got to tear it down.

But there's a problem: Sometimes we leaders believe the same things.

What you believe about volunteers will determine whether those volunteers stay at their current level or grow in leadership and commitment. You may not be able to get folks to grow, but you can sure *stunt* their growth.

I'm going to share four bedrock truths you need to believe if you're going to have a successful volunteer program. The first truth is something you need to believe about God.

Truth #1: God has promised to meet all your needs.

Philippians 4:19 says, "My God will meet all your needs

according to his glorious riches in Christ Jesus."

I went to a Bible college, and while I was there I studied Greek. In Greek that word *all* has an interesting meaning. It means…well, it means "all"…just like it says. God will meet all your needs in Christ Jesus—period.

We pull this verse out to remind ourselves that God provides everything we need for salvation in Jesus. We know God's our provider. He's our strength. But we forget that God will also meet all our ministry needs—*including our need for volunteers*.

When it comes to getting volunteers we tend to say, "Now Lord, I'm the person with the plan. I've got a marketing campaign all figured out. You take care of salvation and I'll handle recruitment." We want to walk in our own strength when it comes to staffing.

At Church On The Move, I need more than 1,100 volunteers to help me pull off children's ministry, so I *know* about needing volunteers. And I know about wanting to run that show myself. But I can't—and you can't, either.

Why? Because recruiting volunteers isn't just about me training enough people for the jobs I have open. It's about God calling faithful people into ministry. That's his job. My job is to remove all the obstacles I can so they can enter into ministry successfully and serve to God's glory.

I can trust God to meet my needs—*and* the needs of my ministry.

Are you praying about your need for volunteers and for the volunteers you have to move along in their faith journeys? For your current crop of folks to want to step up to new challenges? You can beat the drum until your fingers fall off trying to recruit volunteers, but until God speaks to those people's hearts you're just a nuisance that gets ignored.

I'm not saying to give up on recruiting. But if staffing your children's ministry depends on thinking up new recruitment campaigns every month, I say to stop what you're doing. Instead of advertising, use the next thirty days to pray. Tell God you're trusting him to soften hearts toward children. Tell him what you need—*whom* you need—and ask him to convict and inspire folks.

I haven't always trusted God to provide the volunteers I've needed. There was a time I wasn't even certain God knew what he was doing with my volunteers...who were constantly leaving my ministry.

Near the church where I was working in Montgomery, Alabama, there were two Air Force bases and an air war college. Soon after I'd get a volunteer trained, that person would say, "I just got my orders. We're moving to Germany." I'd look up at the ceiling and say, "Why me, Lord? I've got these people trained! They're ready! Why are you taking my volunteers?"

But then I started thanking God that I was part of a revival in Germany—that God was using me to train volunteers he was going to use there. I had to change my attitude, because they weren't *my* volunteers—they were *God's* volunteers. He could use them in Germany if he wanted to. God wasn't going to set me up to fail in Alabama so he could build up the church in Germany.

I could trust God to meet my needs—*including my need for volunteers.*

Do you believe God will give you the people you need to do effective children's ministry? It's true—and some of those volunteers will do ministry as well as you can do it, if you train them right and set them free to do God's will.

Now let's move on to the second truth you must believe.

TRUTH #2: EVERY CHRISTIAN IS CALLED TO DO MINISTRY.

In 1 Peter 2:9 we read, "You are a chosen people, a royal priesthood, a holy nation, a people belonging to God, that you may declare the praises of him who called you out of darkness into his wonderful light."

That means you're called to be a priest, and so is every other Christian in your church. All of them are, including people who are on fire and doing ministry and those you see twice a year at Christmas and Easter. If they're Christians, they're priests.

And what do priests do? *They do the work of ministry.* They're set apart by God to teach. To preach. To serve. To evangelize. To be prophets—pointing things out to the body of Christ. And they're to do it all to glorify God.

But wait a minute...preaching, teaching, evangelizing... that sounds like *your* job description in the church, doesn't it?

If volunteers are doing your job, why will the church board keep you on staff?

Because as a ministry leader, your role is to equip the volunteers in your area to do ministry effectively. You're to be a coach—*not* to do all the ministry yourself.

Now, I know there are people in your church you'd never trust to organize a conference. There are people who can't lead kids in a craft activity without gluing themselves to the carpet. Not everyone can do what you do. But everyone can do *something*. That's an important truth, because it's easy to look at some people and wonder if God really called them to do ministry. They seem long on faults and short on faith.

Listen: If someone has to be perfect to do ministry in your church, you're going to be very lonely on Volunteer Appreciation Night. And come to think of it, you probably shouldn't be doing ministry, either. If perfection is a requirement, I'm in trouble.

When I headed off to Bible college, my hair was too long, I smoked, I played guitar in bars, and I needed to pare down my vocabulary a bit. OK, a *lot*. Nobody was voting me "most likely to succeed in ministry."

But a wise old pastor recruited me to help out, and he put me where I wouldn't do much damage while I grew in my faith and skills. I quit smoking. I got out of the bars and started playing faith-building music in parking lots where lost teenagers hung out. My mentor set my feet on a path that led me to minister to thousands of children. I'm grateful someone saw potential in me and had the patience to help me grow into it.

Are there people in your church who seem to be missing the talents, abilities, gifts, and passions that might make them effective in ministry? Those are people who can serve. I guarantee it—because that's what God's Word says. God says they're part of the priesthood.

And that makes each and every person in your church a potential volunteer for children's ministry. Not everyone should *be* in children's ministry because not everyone has the gifts to be effective there. But if the church is working like it's supposed to work, with everyone doing something instead of just sitting, you're fishing in a bigger pond than you thought. You're not just recruiting among the Faithful Few who sign up for everything;

you're after people who probably aren't doing anything yet.

Why? Because they're priests—just like you.

So everyone has a calling to do something. That's the second thing you need to believe. The next truth about volunteers builds on that…

TRUTH #3: EVERY CHRISTIAN HAS AT LEAST ONE GIFT TO SHARE.

While it's true that everyone can do *something,* not everyone can do the *same* thing. God's given each of us different talents, passions, and abilities. We're not all the same.

I don't want to get in a debate defining what's meant by *spiritual gift.* Are the items listed in places like 1 Corinthians 12; Romans 12:3-8; and Ephesians 4:11 complete or just examples? Does God always build on your natural bent, or does he sometimes give a gift that's in addition to your natural abilities?

I think God can do whatever he wants. That's why he's God and I'm not. I've got opinions, but I think that when Paul wrote about spiritual gifts, he was more concerned about getting Christians to use what God had given them than in defining what he meant by spiritual gifting.

What I know for sure is this: Scripture says we all have at least one ability, interest, or passion to use for ministry. We all get the chance to participate in serving God and one another.

Ephesians 4:8 says, "When he [Jesus] ascended on high, he led captives in his train and gave gifts to men."

Jesus has ascended, and every person in your church is part of mankind. The way I read this verse, every Christian has at least one gift to use in serving others, glorifying God, and building up the body of Christ.

So far I have yet to meet a person who couldn't do something in ministry.

Don't believe me? Think about this: Joni Eareckson Tada is in a wheelchair. Phil Keaggy is missing a finger. Billy Graham has Parkinson's disease. Are you going to tell me that they aren't doing ministry?

The bottom line is this: Every Christian in your church needs to be volunteering for some ministry position, either inside the church or outside in the community. The purpose of that volunteering should be to glorify God. That's Scripture.

Our job is to help people discover who they are in Christ, be faithful in their love for him, and use their unique, God-given abilities.

A few things sometimes get in the way of that happening. They're traps of wrong thinking people fall into. I'm a great example of the first trap.

Trap One: People may not know who they are in Christ.

I remember when I got to Bible college back in the '70s. I was one of the only guys there with a ponytail. I was the only student in my Bible classes who took a smoke break. I realized there were some areas in my life that needed to be changed if I was going to fit in.

So I got busy changing stuff. I cut my hair and went out and bought a leisure suit so I looked like all the up-and-coming preaching students. Pretty soon I not only looked like the other guys, I learned to talk like them.

It wasn't long before I could hold my own in Godly Tones class. You know, where Southern pastors like me learn to say things like "Father Gooooooood, we praaaaisse you." I had it down, friend. I was ready for *prime time.*

But then I realized that God hadn't created me to be an impersonator. He'd created me to be me and wanted me to find out how I could best do ministry and serve him. Boy, I lost that leisure suit in a minute. I quit talking funny. And that's when I got started being effective.

God's goal for me was never to look and sound like everyone else. He wanted me to look and sound like him. To live like him. And to be the most Christlike Jim I could be.

You've got people in your church who are so busy trying to be someone else that they don't know who they are in Christ. They have no idea who God created them to be.

Trap Two: People may not know there's a place for them.

I serve in a big church, and by the time you get to sing a solo you're a good singer. You've got to be. You're looking out at a sanctuary packed with thousands of people, you're working with excellent musicians, and if you haven't had some serious practice you'll faint dead away about the time the spotlight hits you.

So when Leroy, who mostly sings in the shower, hears those solos and considers how he might fit into the church's music ministry, do you think he'll audition for a solo? Or the choir? No way—he knows he's not good enough to hit all those notes. Plus the church isn't about to install a shower stall up on stage so he's in his preferred venue.

Ol' Leroy just decides there's no place for him to serve at church. He's not good enough.

Maybe he can't sing a solo, but you'd better believe I can use him to lead Christmas carols at our December Christmas programs. I can sure use him to help children learn to sing. I can use his love for music a dozen ways—*if* he knows there are other places for him to serve.

How many Leroys have you got sitting in pews because they don't know there's a place for them to serve?

Trap Three: People don't think they're good enough to do ministry.

Every Christian has a skill, ability, or passion that can be used in ministry. It's there. And if you want to change lives for eternity, help people find a place to serve.

Something was said about me that I want to pass on to you. Lots of things have been said about me that I *wouldn't* care to share, but this one touched me. I hope you'll determine that you want it said about you, too.

When I worked at that Montgomery church, we weren't exactly long on resources or personnel. All the folks with obvious skills and gifts had already been snapped up by other ministries in the church. As the children's ministry guy, I got the leftover volunteers.

But that didn't bother me a bit. You know why? Because I knew that God would meet my ministry need for volunteers. I believed that with all my heart. So I looked a little more closely at people who hadn't been recruited for anything yet, and I asked God to show me their potential.

Here's what a woman told someone about my ministry there

in Montgomery: "You know," she said, "Jim found people in the church that nobody else wanted, discovered their gifts, and God used them to do something important."

That's about the nicest thing anyone has ever said about me.

Are they saying that about you? That you're helping people get involved in ministry? Especially people who look at your semipro music team, the polished speakers, and the drama team that looks like it just finished up a Broadway run, and think, "I'll never be skilled enough to do ministry"?

Those are people who spend their entire church lives sitting in the pew. They just don't believe they've got what it takes.

Convince them otherwise.

Of course, there *are* people who need a little time before jumping into the deep end of the ministry pool.

A friend told me about a guy who became a Christian at a campus ministry event back in the '70s. He called my friend and asked if they could talk.

When my friend knocked on this guy's door, it wasn't the new convert who answered. It was a young lady who had obviously just stepped out of a shower and was wearing nothing but a towel. She wandered off into the bedroom to get dressed as the new convert rounded the corner with a big smile.

"I see you met my roommate," he said. "She's great. Let's talk."

They sat down and this newly converted hippie offered my friend a joint. It seemed the new Christian grew and sold marijuana for a living.

My friend gently turned down the joint and the offer of a beer.

"Well," the new convert said, leaning back in a cloud of smoke, "I'm thinking I need to change some things in my life so I can please Jesus, and I want to use those spiritual gifts you guys talked about. Any idea what my gifts are and where I should start making changes?"

The good news: Over the next few months, that young man found a more appropriate roommate and lifestyle and got a job that wouldn't land him in prison. But when my friend told me about the encounter, he confessed that for the first time in his ministry he'd met someone who seemed to have a completely new spiritual gift: the ability to be a bad example.

I wouldn't have put that new Christian in a classroom to teach children, but I'd have gotten him doing *something* in the church. He needed to rely on God and cooperate with the transformation process God had in mind for him.

We're all sinners. If people think they have to wait until they're perfect to volunteer to serve, they'll never volunteer. Jesus took on some pretty questionable characters as his disciples. Let's not communicate that we can't use tax collectors and fishermen when they were good enough for Jesus.

Here's that last foundational truth.

TRUTH #4: EVERY CHRISTIAN HAS A PARTICULAR FUNCTION IN THE BODY OF CHRIST.

In 1 Corinthians 12, Paul paints a great picture for us. He describes how we're all part of the body of Christ. Each part has a different purpose, and for the body to be healthy each part must be in the right place, doing the right thing.

In other words, we all can do *something,* but we all can't do *everything.*

That's an important concept to grasp when you're managing volunteers. Some people shouldn't be in certain jobs. God hasn't given them what it takes to be successful in a specific area…though that won't always stop them from volunteering to do it.

I never again want to work with a children's ministry volunteer who thinks everything in life should be calm, lined up in straight rows, and silent. People wired like that cannot *survive* in children's ministry. They make great accountants, but they go nuts in the preschool room.

The fact is, there are people who shouldn't work with kids. I don't want them as volunteers no matter how called they feel. It's going to be a terrible experience for them, the kids, and me if they ever find their way into a classroom.

Boy, you can see those folks coming a mile away, can't you? They show up in your office with a grim little thin-lipped smile and announce that the Lord has revealed to them that it's their job to straighten out the problem the church is having with children.

The biggest problem, of course, is that the problem they want to solve isn't a problem you think needs to be solved.

They want to make certain kids can recite the books of the Bible forward and backward. You want kids to love Jesus more.

They want to train kids to sit quietly and not distract adults. You want to train kids to serve Jesus and distract the world with enthusiastic faith.

They want kids to become little adults. You want adults to have childlike faith.

Buddy, when someone comes rolling at you like a bulldozer, carrying an agenda for what needs to be changed, that person probably isn't called to children's ministry. God calls people who love kids and who want kids to love Jesus.

If you want volunteers to stick in your ministry, you've got to get them in the right jobs. Don't stick an eyeball on the bottom of a leg and expect it to be a foot. No amount of training is going to fix *that* problem.

PUT THEM TOGETHER AND WHAT DO YOU GET?

Let me summarize:
- God has promised to meet all your needs.
- Every Christian is supposed to be in ministry.
- Every Christian has at least one God-given ability, interest, or passion to use in ministry. And...
- Every Christian is designed to function somewhere in the body of Christ.

Sounds like you're sitting on a gold mine of volunteers, doesn't it? Since everyone in your church is supposed to serve somewhere, there should be a long line of people just *waiting* to help out in children's ministry.

But that's not how it usually goes.

If we could claim any Scripture verse for volunteers, I'd choose Matthew 22:14: "Many are called, but few are chosen" (King James Version). I want my pick of the best of the best. Children deserve to be served by the best volunteers we can find.

But the verse we're usually handed is a paraphrase of a line pulled out of Mark 8:34: Whosoever will come, let them come.

We're often just looking for *bodies*. If people are standing and breathing, we figure we can train them. And that's exactly the wrong way to think about volunteers, especially if you want volunteers who'll stick.

Your biggest temptation—and it'll become your biggest problem if you give in—is to take people who are willing to serve but who haven't been given the right abilities to work with kids.

God equips those he calls to a ministry, but he doesn't necessarily equip people who just happen to be available and willing to help. Do you see the difference? You're looking for volunteers who have God-given abilities and aptitudes that will let them function well in children's ministry—and that will help them feel fulfilled as they serve alongside you.

You're *not* looking for people who just happen to have nothing better to do, so they sign up.

So how do you do it? How do you get excellent volunteers who'll stick with you? What's your next step? Running a big recruitment campaign?

Nope. It's to tweak your thinking a bit more. It's to begin looking at volunteers not as people with little jobs to do but as people who have volunteer *careers*.

It's taking volunteering in your church to the next level. It's developing a structure that lets volunteers grow and mature, giving them the opportunity to get better at what they do.

Let's talk about what volunteer careers look like and how encouraging them can help you find Velcro volunteers who stick.

chapter 3

Volunteer Careers

To keep volunteers long term you've got to give them more than just jobs—they need careers that involve significant ministry. Here's how to make that happen.

I want to tell you about the worst job I ever had.

Now, I've had my share of awful jobs—jobs I wouldn't wish on anyone. But I've been earning my own spending money since I was ten, and I was never too proud to earn an honest dollar if the chance came by.

I outran dogs when I was a paperboy and scraped bugs off windshields when I was pumping gas. I counted furniture during inventories, and for a couple of years I slung bedpans as an orderly in an emergency room.

I've done magic shows at kids' birthday parties. I taught guitar lessons to people who never seemed to practice. I delivered flowers—which is no fun at all when they're for funerals.

But the worst job of all—the smelliest, nastiest, hardest dollar I've ever earned—was as the dishwasher at a Boy Scout camp. I was the *only* dishwasher. For breakfast, lunch, and dinner.

I took that job thinking it couldn't be too hard to wash dishes. And it isn't—if you're washing them for yourself or a family. But when you're trying to stay ahead of a crowd of Boy Scouts, it's an uphill battle every inch of the way.

All summer long I dragged myself out of bed early and stayed up late so I could spray dishes with scalding water. I stood in wet shoes, up to my elbows in water that had long ago turned to muck. I sang songs to take my mind off the job. I'd think about something else—*anything* else—and count the days until summer ended and I could walk out of that steaming kitchen.

I wasn't even a *Christian,* and I prayed for deliverance.

The worst thing about that job, other than having to scrape dried macaroni and cheese off white dinner plates, was that I was *stuck.* Once I'd mastered the fundamentals of dishwashing, it's not like I could get promoted. I was the only dishwasher there. Taking that job was not a smart career move.

After a couple days of getting the routine down, the rest of the summer was long, hot, and boring. It was worse than a dead-end job—as soon as someone found cheap enough paper plates and plastic silverware, I wasn't going to have any job at all.

Buddy, that's when you know you've got no future: when you can be replaced by stuff on the shelf at the grocery store!

What made that job so awful? Apart from the heat and the smell, that is?

I was bored.

Stuck standing in front of a sink, hosing down dishes, locked in place by a job you hate—that's when you start to understand why some people talk to themselves. And why eventually they start to answer back.

I couldn't change jobs.

Nobody in his right mind wanted to trade jobs with me. The guy who worked outside mowing the grass wasn't about to swap. The lifeguards weren't interested in job sharing. I was stuck. Period.

Nobody invested in me.

Here's the thing about hiring a dishwasher at a Boy Scout camp: You don't expect to hang on to him. You know that when the summer is over he's going to get out of there as fast as his soggy shoes will carry him.

So you don't worry about long-term career development. You don't send your dishwasher to the Advanced Dishwasher Seminar or buy him that bestselling book, *Better Dishwashing: Your Ticket to Success.*

You just want someone who'll stick it out until fall. Then,

next summer, you hire someone else desperate enough to take the job.

No *wonder* I grew to hate that job.

Now, here's a question for you: How many of your volunteers are in the same spot I was in—bored, stuck, and sure nobody is willing to invest in them?

"But Brother Jim," you're saying, "I'd never treat my volunteers that way!"

Really?

When's the last time you asked volunteers who have held the same jobs for a while if they're bored? When was the last time you promoted a volunteer? The last time you actually *helped* one of your children's ministry volunteers change jobs and go help out in the youth department for a spell?

Are your volunteers stuck?

They won't tell you, you know. They'll gut it out because that's what we're supposed to do—suffer for the cause of Christ down there in children's church. But I'll tell you this: I don't want the kids in my church being served by adults who consider volunteering a chore. I want volunteers who are delighted to be serving. That attitude will be communicated to the kids.

THE STORY OF MARY BETH AND THE ROLLRITE WIDGET COMPANY

Mary Beth's first job out of school was in the mailroom of the Rollrite Widget Company. A steady paycheck, good benefits— she was glad to land the job. But do you think she wants to be in that same job when she retires in forty years?

Of course not! A mailroom job is fine—and I'm glad there are people who process mail—but if she's still stuck in that mailroom two years from now, she'll go find a more challenging job down the street.

You see, Mary Beth wants a *career*—not just a job. She wants to keep learning new things and building new skills. She's doesn't want a dead-end job.

Her first week in the mailroom, Mary Beth was worse than useless. Having her around actually slowed things down, because she didn't know what she was doing. Plus she kept interrupting everyone with questions.

But by week three she was flying high. She'd mastered the job and gotten the place organized. Inside of six months she had the mail prioritized, the work systemized, and the job customized. And if someone had given Mary Beth a computer, that mailroom would've been *digitized*. The mail was moving more quickly than ever before, and even Mr. Rollrite stopped in to shake her hand.

Now, several things could happen for Mary Beth at this point...

1. Her boss might realize she's a top performer and look for new places to use Mary Beth. He might promote her to director of mailing and packaging. Being a supervisor would keep her learning new skills as she mastered a bigger job and worked with people.

2. Mary Beth might transfer to another department. Sales, maybe, or widget engineering. Some place she'd learn new things and keep from being bored. It wouldn't necessarily be more money, but it *would* be a step in her career.

3. Her boss could decide she was the best mailroom worker he'd ever seen and leave her right where she was—and risk losing her as Mary Beth grew tired of doing the same old thing, day after day.

Any good supervisor would see that Mary Beth was an employee Rollrite Widget didn't want to lose and help her be content by giving Mary Beth growth opportunities.

The Story of Mary Beth and Your Church

Mary Beth doesn't work at the Widget Company on weekends. In fact, every Sunday she volunteers in your children's ministry. And here's something you might not know: *Mary Beth wants a career at church, too.*

She wants to grow in her skills, learn new things, and not be stuck in a dead-end job on Sundays just as much as when she punches the time clock on Monday morning.

You can't ask Mary Beth to help out in junior church and

expect her to be happy forever. Maybe she does a bang-up job and you see kids praising God when she leads the songs. You can tell she finds it rewarding to work with that group of kids. She's in a volunteer job that makes good use of her temperament, spiritual gifts, skills, abilities, and passion for worship.

Just the same, eventually she'll want to try something new.

And if you're supervising her, you've got pretty much the same choices her boss at Rollrite Widget has:

1. You can realize you've got a top-performing volunteer who's done great things in junior church. You can talk with her and see if she'll spread her wings and take on more responsibility. Maybe you'll promote her to junior church director and have her supervise some other volunteers.

2. If she wants, you might move her over to the Sunday school side of things where she can do something new. Put her in a classroom with the fifth grade boys. She won't be bored, that's for sure.

3. Or you can leave her right where she is. Be happy you've got a great junior church worker. But don't be surprised when she up and quits on you to volunteer in another ministry area at your church or in another church altogether.

Mary Beth isn't just looking for a *job* at church. She wants a *career*.

"Career volunteers"—people who have a heart for serving others and a desire to use and grow in their skills—are worth their weight in gold. They're almost always your top-performing people. You want as many of them as you can find—or create.

That's right—*create*. Because how long someone sticks as a volunteer, and how much that person grows, has a lot to do with you. As a children's ministry leader, you can encourage volunteers to stay long term, or you can send them scrambling for the exit signs.

Here's how it works: First you build a volunteer-friendly culture. Then you put in place the other things that are required for volunteers to thrive and grow—I'll tell you what those things are as you move through this book. That's when you find that volunteers start to hang around longer. They don't just take a job and keep it until they get bored. They begin to desire and accept more responsibility and get involved in finding solutions, not just pointing out problems.

They become *career* volunteers whose involvement deepens and whose service stretches out over years or even decades.

You want to see that happen? Of course you do—and I'll tell you how to encourage it. But first, let me define what I mean by a volunteer "career."

WHAT'S A VOLUNTEER "CAREER"?

I know the term *career* bothers some folks. It sounds a little too businesslike for church work. If church workers are concerned about their "careers," are they really putting God and his work first? In fact, wouldn't we be doing God a favor if we weeded people out who want something for themselves when they follow Jesus?

What we need are volunteers who have their whole hearts in it! Volunteers who aren't afraid to give all! Volunteers like the twelve disciples!

Well, like *some* of the twelve disciples anyway…

We wouldn't want volunteers like James and John. Those ol' boys had some serious career issues—and they created morale problems on the team too.

One time James and John had their *mama* go with them to see Jesus. The Bible doesn't tell us if it was her idea or theirs, but the three of them knelt down and that woman actually asked Jesus if her boys could sit next to him in his kingdom.

I think that proves she was a Southern mama, because it didn't bother her any to speak her mind. She figured if Jesus was going to have a favorite disciple, it ought to be one of her boys. And if he could have one favorite, he could just as easily have two. And that's where she saw her boys: as Jesus' favorites.

Jim could sit by Jesus' right hand, and Johnny could sit next to Jesus' left elbow. The table of honor. The catbird seats. That's where she expected to see *her* sons. And Jim and Johnny let her do the asking.

Here's what the Bible says about the impact of that conversation on the rest of the team: "When the ten heard about this, they were indignant with the two brothers" (Matthew 20:24).

You *think*? Twelve guys following Jesus and two of them sneak in an application for the "head disciple" job. The other guys didn't even know that job was *open*.

For the Zebedee boys and their mama, I think this was a career move, pure and simple. Get in good with the boss and he'll remember you when he makes it big. And they had to act fast before Peter got the inside track.

This is an example of what we're afraid of when we talk about careers in the church—that ambition will overtake discipleship and service. That people will sign up to work in the church nursery so they can sell cosmetics to the women who are rocking infants instead of signing up so they can serve babies.

And sometimes that happens.

But even for James and John, it worked out. The Holy Spirit got hold of their hearts, and they had lengthy careers serving Jesus—first as followers, then as witnesses, then as leaders. The job descriptions changed, but the remainder of their lives were careers of service. And I don't know where they're sitting in heaven, but I've got to believe they can slide in beside Jesus now and then if they want a word.

My point: "Career" doesn't have to equal "selfish ambition." Even people who start slow can finish strong.

When you're talking about volunteers, a "career" is simply a progression of jobs that keeps someone growing and stretching. It's what gives people who have been faithful in small things the chance to be faithful in bigger things.

That's what we're after, isn't it? For every Christian to find a place to serve and to keep growing in service until Jesus comes back or the Christian goes to be with Jesus? The fundamental beliefs discussed in Chapter 2—that every Christian is called to ministry, that every Christian has at least one gift to share, and that every Christian has a particular function in the body of Christ—all point to Christians having a life of service to God and the church.

And doesn't it make sense that as Christians mature they're able to serve in new ways?

I keep hammering on how volunteers need to have volunteer careers because it's such a hard concept for some Christian leaders to grasp. They say, "Brother Jim, Christians just need to follow

Jesus. When people follow Jesus they don't get bored. I'll discern where people need to serve in the church's ministry, and it's up to people to be satisfied in their service."

Two problems with that:

1. People do get bored. They *do* expect that they'll be fulfilled in their ministries. Sorry, but that's human nature, and I for one don't think it's unreasonable.

2. As a Christian leader, I'm not the only one who can discern the will of God. When someone on my team comes to me and tells me she thinks God wants her to serve in another area, I don't argue the point. I bless her and help her make the transition any way I can. Why? Because she's probably right. She's been praying about it. I trust her spiritual maturity, or she wouldn't be on my team in the first place.

And if she's wrong—if she gets over to the church office and discovers she'd much rather change diapers than answer phones—I want her to know she can come back to work in the nursery.

Two Ways to Do Career Planning

Back when I was in high school, you got called to the guidance office for one of two reasons. The first was to get a talking to about stuff you'd been doing—the stuff they'd caught you at or the stuff they were pretty sure you'd done but there weren't any witnesses.

The second reason was to help you figure out what to do with your life.

I'll leave it up to you as to which reason usually had me trudging down to the guidance office. But *this* particular time I was there to figure out what to do with my life.

The counselor was a nice woman, but she was tired. She'd been doing this a long time. And from the look on her face you could tell not many kids took her advice.

My file was open on her desk, and she'd sorted through the test results, teachers' comments, my grades, and whatever else was in there. She wanted to help me settle on a career to pursue after I graduated.

But I didn't need *her* help to know what I was doing after

high school. I was going to join the Rolling Stones and make an obscene amount of money playing guitar. I'd been playing guitar for money for years already, I knew every song the Stones ever recorded, and I figured it was just a matter of time until Keith Richards keeled over and I got hired on as his replacement. It could happen any minute. I kept a bag packed.

And if *that* didn't work out, I could always go play football in college.

The whole conversation didn't last long, and that poor lady went home looking even more tired.

See, she thought having a career meant you sat down when you were seventeen years old and mapped out your entire life. You decided what you wanted to do for a living and then backed into a plan that would get you there. The rest of your life you just followed the plan.

That's the first way to do career planning: You put a seventeen-year-old in charge of your life. Even at seventeen, that one scared me. I barely knew what I'd be doing the next *day* let alone the rest of my life. Plus I was wired to do career planning the way most people do it: hopscotch around trying lots of stuff before finally settling into something. I call that the "Well, What About *This*?" approach to career planning.

There are people who know exactly what they'll do decades in advance, but I have no idea how they do it. ("First I'll be a junior account representative, then an account representative, then a regional account manager, then a junior sales VP, then the VP of sales, then I'll take over the company when I'm fifty-nine.") That's just not how my life works. For most of us, our careers include lots of experiments and sudden left turns.

I'm all for planning. I'm a *fanatic* about planning; just ask people who work with me at Church On The Move. I've got a spreadsheet for everything. But I know that when it comes to crafting a career, that's not really my job.

My job is to be faithful in following God's leading. Along the way I'll pick up skills and abilities I can use to serve him. I'll come in contact with people God wants me to meet. And while all the zigs and zags may look crazy on paper, in the end it'll all make sense.

You see, when you're here on earth as Jesus' ambassador, he

figures he can move you around. I don't think Jesus is a big respecter of our plans. He figures that if we're his, we're *his*. He can use us wherever he wants us.

So I don't get surprised when someone who used to be a teacher and then became a stockbroker but now sells satellite phones signs up to help out with my children's program. I don't see those job changes as a sign of instability at all. I figure I know where to borrow some telephones for our next retreat. And I expect just as much bouncing around when it comes to a person's volunteer career, too.

I don't get discouraged when I hear that a person signing up for children's ministry spent time as a Big Brother, then a scout leader, and then a Sunday school teacher. That all works for me. I don't get offended that he volunteered "outside the church." It's all good—I just want to know what he learned along the way and why God's leading him in our direction.

Do this: When you're interviewing volunteers (and you will; we'll talk about that in Chapter 7), ask about their *career* in volunteering. Don't just ask about what they've done in a children's ministry inside the walls of a church on Sunday mornings. Ask about how God used them when they were a Big Brother or Big Sister or leading a scout troop.

As for me, I *love* having former scout leaders come serve with us. Those people have moved a dozen kids through the woods and up mountains; I know that taking the preschoolers down the hall for a potty break won't be a big challenge for them.

And by the way, if Mick Jagger is reading this, I want him to know the offer stands: Give me the word and I'll join the Stones for a tour. I'll need Saturdays and Sundays off so I can work with kids at my church, but to make up for it I'll help haul out equipment after the shows. Call me. We'll talk.

How to Encourage Volunteer Careers in Children's Ministry

If everything went according to *my* plan, here's how children's ministry volunteers would move through the ranks at my church…

First, they'd serve in a small capacity so we could get to know them. We want to be sure they're compatible with our culture and that they're faithful. I don't care if the person was the supervisor of children's ministries in another church. Titles don't impress me. I want to know if a volunteer is someone kids in my care can look up to and model their lives after. If so, we're in business. If not, that volunteer is removed from the program until issues are resolved.

Second, we'd work with that person to develop his or her skills. We'd zero in on what could be improved and provide the resources needed to take skills to the next level. We'd have that volunteer delighted with the growth he or she experienced.

Third, we'd work on leadership skills. Can this volunteer be a leader of ten other people? of twenty? of fifty? If so, what will it take to get the volunteer prepared for leadership? We'd work on that.

Fourth, we'd keep checking to see what the Lord is telling the volunteer. Is it time to take another step in leadership? To move into a different area of children's ministry? To reduce responsibilities for a season because of the stress of a new job, a sick parent, or a new baby in the house?

If things went according to my plan, volunteers would stick in children's ministry for at least ten years. And volunteers would be growing and challenged the entire time.

But God's plan for volunteers doesn't always match my plan. The Lord giveth and the Lord taketh away. Sometimes a volunteer I think I can't live without gets transferred to a new job a thousand miles away. Or that wonderful nursery worker gets blessed with twins that keep her plenty busy with babies at home.

I want to always encourage volunteers to do what God tells them to do, even if that means leaving children's ministry. But while they're with me, I'm going to do what I can to help them stick until God calls them elsewhere. I want effective, long-term volunteers, and following are the four things I do to get them.

I'd suggest you do the same four things yourself.

1. We bring the right volunteers on board.

How you select and place volunteers is critical. If you pick people who'll fit into your culture and who are committed to your vision and mission statements, you're ahead of the game.

In the long run, it's better to leave a volunteer job open than fill it with the wrong volunteer.

I'll tell you later how to make sure the people you get in jobs are the right people for those jobs, but for now let me just say this: If you get someone into a job where he or she is unhappy and a bad fit, it chases away people who would do a better job. Nobody wins—not you, the volunteers, or the kids you want to serve.

2. We let people do what God's wired them to do.

Can I confess something here? I love doing children's ministry, and I've enjoyed all of it. I've run puppet ministries, led music, preached children's sermons, taught classes, and fixed the soundboard. I've counseled kids and their families.

But I'll confess right here and now, in front of God and you, that I'm not a crafty kind of guy. My wife doesn't encourage me to build a lot of things with my hands around our house. She's always saying things like "Honey, let's hire someone to get that new kitchen shelf done. You're so busy."

What she really *means* is "I want to be sure that when I put dishes on the shelf it won't fall off the wall." My handiwork has earned that kind of reputation.

You leave me in a room with a bunch of third-graders, a glue gun, and some craft sticks, and no matter how much I intend to build Noah's ark, I'm gonna burn down your church building. I'm just not wired to run the craft room at vacation Bible school. So if you want me to stick around as a volunteer, you'd better figure out a way to let me avoid that job. I won't stick in a place that sets me up to fail.

And since you asked, the cantata is my least favorite art form, so count me out if you've got one scheduled at Christmas, even if you think all children's leaders need to be involved. Ditto for bell choir; I think bell choirs are the number one cause of hair loss in the church, and they should be outlawed.

Anything else? Hmmm...oh, yes: If we do a living nativity, can I be the guy who takes care of the donkey? I know Mary gets to ride it in the play, her being pregnant and all, but I'd like to take it for a spin around the parking lot after the crowd leaves.

I'm a versatile guy. You'd *love* having me volunteer at your children's ministry. There's hardly anything I won't do if it makes a kid happy and helps that kid get to know Jesus.

But there are still things I don't do well or that I dislike doing. *And that's true of every one of your volunteers.* If you've got each Sunday school teacher preparing and teaching a lesson, leading songs, praying out loud, leading discussions, *and* doing follow-up, you may well have a situation where teachers love parts of their jobs and hate other parts of their jobs.

Will those teachers stick around as long-term volunteers? Probably not.

Let people do what they do well. Let them off the hook for doing things they can't do well. Just because ventriloquism came easy to you doesn't mean it'll be easy for everyone to learn and use in class.

In our interview process, we let volunteers tell us flat out what they like and dislike doing. We *ask* what people can and can't do because we take God at his word that he gives different gifts to different people. If that's true, how can we expect everyone to be good at the same things?

3. We notice volunteers and keep noticing them.

Have you ever bought a new car? There's nothing that'll get your self-esteem inflated like walking into the showroom of a car dealership.

Those salespeople couldn't be happier to see you. They act like they've been waiting for you ever since the dealership opened. They shake your hand, usher you around, use your name every fifteen seconds, and if you want a soft drink it's yours—no charge.

I think we'd put half the counselors in our town out of business if people would just stop by car dealerships now and then.

Of course, once they figure out you really *are* just looking, car salespeople act like you're not even there. So maybe those counselors shouldn't close up shop just yet.

My point: You can't pour all kinds of attention on incoming volunteers and then ignore them after they're signed up. That communicates your ministry is all about getting new volunteers, not keeping old ones. Noticing volunteers isn't just about sending thank-you cards. It includes training and evaluation, too.

More about that in Chapter 8.

4. We provide growth opportunities.

If you're a volunteer in our church and you do a great job, we're going to be asking you if there's something more you want to do. We're going to invest in you with training and coaching. We'll help you reach the next level in your skills and responsibilities.

And you know who gets to spearhead that effort? If you're the person in charge of your church's children's ministry, it's you.

I love working with kids and make sure I still get time with them, but these days I mostly train adults who go work with kids. Long ago I decided not to fight God on this one. I want to pour my heart into those grown-ups just as much as I've poured my heart into kids.

God may be calling you into a similar role in your church: to coach, mentor, and promote people when they're ready.

If you're in a small church, there may be no new job to promote people into. You're in charge, and there are three people who work with you. That's it.

Do this: Give away some of your job to keep things interesting for those three volunteers. Include them in decision making. Ask them their opinions—and listen. Look for ways you can give them chances to take the ball and run. Send them to a church you respect for a training or mentoring session.

And in time you may run into the same problem I have: Other churches keep wanting to hire away my volunteers!

That's it. It's not rocket science, is it? Anybody could do the things that are required to establish volunteers in their ministries, make them successful, and develop a significant number of them into long-term leaders.

So why is it so rare?

I'll tell you why: It requires structure, and it requires discipline.

Structure

We children's workers aren't real big on structure. We're people lovers, and our experience working with kids has proven that our plans can fall apart in a heartbeat. We learn to value flexibility and thinking on our feet.

The problem is that pretty soon we're *always* being flexible. We're *always* making things up as we go. We set structure and planning aside and never get back to them.

If you want your volunteers to stick—to find so much joy, fulfillment, and significance in their volunteering that you'd have to pry them away from your children's ministry—you need structure.

You need to provide structured

- *interviews and placement* so volunteers land in the right jobs,
- *job descriptions* so volunteers know what they're supposed to do,
- *supervision* so volunteers aren't left wandering around in the wilderness,
- *evaluations* so volunteers know if they're being successful,
- *training* so volunteers become comfortable in their roles and experts in their areas of service, and
- *growth opportunities* so volunteers have careers—not just jobs.

The remainder of this book will walk you through how to establish those structures in your ministry. Whether you've got five volunteers or five hundred, you need these structures in place. It's essential.

Discipline

Structure doesn't mean much if you never make use of it. So get yourself a calendar and some file folders, and create a file for each volunteer.

When will you evaluate each volunteer? What training does each volunteer need? What training has each volunteer already *had*? Who's supervising whom?

Are you collecting data on attendance so you know how many kids each teacher is caring for in class? How many years each volunteer has been active in the church and active in children's ministry? The data you need to manage a volunteer doesn't just assemble itself; you've got to pull it together and organize it so it's useful.

And then you've got to do the things that are required for hanging on to top performers, whether they're volunteers or employees.

While there's a *lot* I'd never want to copy from secular companies, I think they've got us cold on this one. They understand the importance of spotting talent and dedication and giving those people a career instead of just a job.

Smart companies have figured out how to hang on to their top producers.

How the Big Boys Do It

Human resource professionals in successful companies go to great lengths to keep top performers around.

It makes sense. In most companies there are a few jobs where it takes five or six months for a new person to begin hauling his or her weight. Those months are spent learning the ropes, studying the business, and getting to know the staff.

No wonder a company that hires a new VP doesn't want to do it very often. It's expensive and time consuming. If there's a great person in place, it's far less costly to keep that person than to replace him or her.

That's true of your volunteers, too. There are jobs—like folding the bulletin covers—where you can have someone trained and effective in about five minutes. But there are also jobs where it's a *huge* investment of time and energy to get someone to the point where he or she is truly effective. Try to train a person to run your preschool department in five minutes and see what happens. It's not going to be pretty.

Here's what companies do to keep top performers on board and happy. What would happen if you treated your top volunteers the same way?

Top performers are treated well.

I'm not talking about throwing extra money at people. A

paycheck is no guarantee that top employees will stick around.

What I do mean is that those folks feel heard and valued. That now and then the Big Boss swings by and says, "I'm glad you're here. Thanks for your contributions."

These folks get the tools they need to be effective. If they need information, it's provided. If they need a new computer to run new software, it shows up on their desk. And when they're evaluated, close attention is paid to how they're getting along with their supervisors.

The employee-supervisor relationship is *the* key to making work a comfortable place. You may work in the world's best company, but if you don't get along with your direct supervisor...well, you won't be happy. And sooner or later, you'll leave. Probably sooner.

So let me ask this about your top-performing volunteers—the ones who are passionate, gifted, and committed. The ones you'd hate to see leave:

- Do they have a say in things?
- Do they hear a word of thanks and appreciation from the children's pastor now and then?
- Are you taking care of their classrooms or work areas so your volunteers are comfortable and content?
- How do they get along with the people who supervise them?

THE WORST BOSS EXERCISE

Sometime ask volunteers who report to you to share a story about the worst boss they've ever had. Caution them not to use names—that person may be in your church!

Listen closely. Ask lots of questions so you understand exactly what made those bosses so horrible. Then ask yourself: "In what ways do those bosses resemble me?"

If there are similarities and you want to hang on to those volunteers, you've got some changing to do.

Top performers aren't allowed to get stale.

Your top people usually like a challenge now and then. Not all of them, but most. That's why they're your top performers.

In a workplace, these are the people who get put on cross-departmental teams or take on extra projects. They still do their own jobs, but they get a crack at doing something new, too.

The result: They get to scratch their itch to explore new

things in the company—not by going out and getting new jobs. And the company gets the benefit of their energy and out-of-the-box thinking.

Now—about your volunteers...

- Are they given the chance to stretch and grow?
- Are you tapping the very best they have to offer?
- What would happen if you invited them to put their heads together and tackle one of those big problems you can't seem to fix, like how to get VBS kids to come to Sunday school or how to do adequate follow-up with visitors?

Top performers are kept in the loop.

You make sure these folks don't get surprised by a change in policy or reorganization. You have regular "touch base" meetings so there's an ongoing information flow. Communicating seems like a little thing—until you don't do it.

Remember: Your top volunteers are probably already leaders, whether or not they've got the official position. They influence other volunteers. It's smart to give top volunteers the information they need to lead effectively and stop rumors from circulating.

- Do you regularly meet with your top volunteers? How often? For what purpose? Are you sharing the information they need?
- Do you recognize top volunteers as leaders? Who's following them? Are they heading the direction you want them to go?

Top performers get training.

I'm lucky—we hold leadership and training events at my church, so it's easy to get my top volunteers here. They don't have to travel across the country or take vacation time to attend.

But I'll tell you—it's worth getting your folks trained no matter how many hurdles you've got to jump through to make it happen.

Training keeps your sharp people sharp, especially if you ask folks who attend conferences and classes to come back and pass along what they've learned. You've got to understand material at an entirely deeper level if you're going to teach it, so everyone

   children's ministry volunteers that stick

on your team wins when conference attendees give a report.

And you train top people not just for the job they have now. You train them for the *next* job they want in your ministry. You don't promote people without checking with them first and getting them ready.

Doris may be the best Sunday school teacher you've ever met. Parents stop you in the hallway and tell you how their kids love her, and they're learning bunches. You wish you had a dozen more teachers just like Doris.

So you promote her to a master teacher coordinator. You tell her she'll be rotating through other classrooms, evaluating and critiquing other teachers. Because Doris trusts you know what's best for the ministry, she agrees.

And in a year she's gone. She's no longer a volunteer. Or it works the other way: No sooner does Doris evaluate a teacher and that person quits.

What happened?

The train could have run off the track lots of places, but here's what I suspect: You didn't train Doris how to train other teachers. Doris had tremendous kid skills, but she wasn't comfortable critiquing and coaching peers. Either she felt totally ineffective and quit, or she charged in like a bull in a china shop and every teacher she worked with quit.

Either way you lose Doris—and maybe other volunteers, too.

What would it have cost you to get Doris hooked up with a mentor who could teach her how to coach others? You could have found someone who did the same thing in the public schools, or you could have sent her to a class. I'm sure the cost of the training would have been far less than the cost of your time spent replacing her.

Top performers get promoted.

I understand that in small churches it's hard to come up with new jobs for your top people. You don't want six master teachers and one new recruit who gets coached half to death.

But you can increase job responsibilities without changing titles. Just revise job descriptions so your volunteers are getting new challenges and opportunities to shine.

So we're agreed that your volunteers need careers, right? And you're ready to reap the benefits of having long-term volunteers who are growing in their skills?

Then let's go find them for you.

chapter 4

Right People, Right Places, Right Time, Right Reasons

Want volunteers to stick? Then make sure they're the right people
in the right places at the right time for the right reasons.

I once saw a movie (*For Richer or Poorer,* PG-13) that reminded
me of volunteering at church. The movie's not actually *about*
that, of course. It's about a spoiled, married couple hiding out
from the Internal Revenue Service on an Amish farm.

Tim Allen and Kirstie Alley star as a Manhattan couple living
on credit. They're on the verge of divorce when the IRS comes
after them for back taxes, their dishonest accountant hightails it
to Europe, and Allen and Alley are left holding the bag.

And that bag is *empty.*

So the couple escapes to Amish country where they pretend
to be cousins of an Amish family living on a farm. They say
they're volunteers who have come to help with spring planting,
so the family takes them in.

Here's the thing: Allen and Alley know nothing about farm-
ing—or about manual labor, for that matter. Suddenly they're
expected to do a lot of both. It doesn't go smoothly.

What I saw, beyond all the slapstick, was that these two
volunteers were the *wrong* people in the *wrong* place at the
wrong time for all the *wrong* reasons.

That combination happens way too often in church, too. We

look at our volunteers and see people who want to quit, or they're complainers, or they're plugging away even though they're miserable.

What happened? How did something that's supposed to be a joy turn into such drudgery?

It's usually this: We've got the wrong people in the wrong places at the wrong time for the wrong reasons. Get any one of those factors out of whack and it's a recipe for disaster.

Don't believe me? Let's take a look at what happens when...

You get the *wrong* people...

Who are you looking for as a volunteer in your children's ministry? Do you have a profile of what a "right person" would look like? If not, how will you know one when you see one? How will you tell the difference between a "right person" and a "wrong person"?

I'm pretty quick to invite people to volunteer for children's ministry. I don't do much recruiting—I *draft* people to serve. I'll tell you more about that in Chapter 5.

I can draft folks in part because I've learned over the years what people who'll thrive in children's ministry look and sound like. What they value. How they're wired. I can pretty much tell who'll fit after talking with someone for a few minutes.

Plus there's a safety net: I'm going to run a background check on everyone who fills out an application. I'll do an interview. If I misjudged someone, that'll be caught before we offer someone a volunteer job.

I just want to get a discussion started about volunteering so I can get some people in the pipeline. I want to find interested people—if they work out for children's ministry, great. If I end up referring them elsewhere to serve in the church, that's fine, too.

But I know this: I can't turn a volunteer into a volunteer who *sticks* until that person volunteers in the first place. And few people volunteer until they're asked to do so.

In one sense, there's no such thing as a "wrong" person for volunteering. As we discussed earlier, 1 Corinthians 12 says that every believer has a ministry. We all can do something; we just can't all do *everything*. Some folks need help figuring out where they're the right person to serve...and where they're the wrong person.

In children's ministry the wrong people are people who aren't fully committed to our ministry's vision and mission. They're people who don't have the patience or energy to work with kids. They're people who sign up because they prey on children. They're people who fall short of living a life that's a model for children. They're people who don't have the mix of skills, passion, and temperament that make them effective.

Listen—it's *always* better to leave a volunteer spot open than to fill it with the wrong person. Wrong people cost you in three ways:

1. They take forever to train.

Why? *Because they're the wrong people.* God didn't intend for them to serve where you've put them. If you find yourself hammering a square peg into a round hole and it's slow going, don't blame the peg or the hammer. It's your fault.

2. They often don't do a very good job.

But if you've got the wrong person in a job, what do you expect?

Now and then my wife and daughters give me a little dose of culture. They dress me up and take me downtown to watch a ballet.

And I fit right into that audience. I clean up as best as I can, and I'm on my best behavior. I pay attention, clap in all the right places, and to look at me you'd think I was raised on ballet. I do my family proud at those events.

I'm absolutely the right guy for the audience. But that doesn't mean I'm the right guy to run backstage, slip on tights, and come out to dance.

I know how to find my way up on stage. I can figure out how to pull on a pair of tights—it can't be that complicated. But I wouldn't come out on stage and do a pirouette the way it's supposed to be done. And the audience would be looking for refunds even before I got to the part of the ballet where I try to catch a couple of those ballerinas who always seem to be launching themselves at the guys.

I just don't have the talent or training to dance ballet. It's not that I *won't* do it; I *can't* do it. Me being willing has nothing to do with it. I've got the hang time of a rock. If I went leaping across the stage, it would look like I was trying to tackle somebody.

3. They keep the right people from participating.

You've only got so many volunteer jobs to fill. Maybe it's a thousand, maybe it's ten. Whatever the number, you want the best possible people in those jobs because your ministry will never be better than the people serving in it.

And that puts you in a delicate spot: How do you know who's the best person for each job? And what happens if someone who's clearly not the best person signs up?

For starters, know that by "best" I don't mean smartest, most handsome, or best dressed. I mean most appropriate because of skills, abilities, passion, and gifting. I'll honor how God's wired people no matter how they look.

And here's how you know who's best for each job: *You interview them.* All of them. Every volunteer in your program and every person entering your program as a volunteer. I'll tell you how in Chapter 7. You sort out where people belong, get them placed, then watch them as they're trained and launched in their volunteer ministry. That lets you confirm that your discernment (and theirs) was right.

But if your jobs are all filled by the wrong people, where are you going to put that new, gifted person who's going to have a great ministry with the kids? Nowhere, that's where. And that new person won't bother asking about signing up because there aren't any jobs open.

This is going to make you uncomfortable, but here it is: If you start running your volunteer program the right way, you may have to ask some people to find other ministries.

I don't care if Millie Mae has been teaching junior church since Moses was a guest speaker. If her idea of staying current is using a tie-dyed flannel graph instead of a blue one, she's got to go. She can go get some training to update her presentation skills, or she can go to the toddler class where the kids will love playing with little cutout Bible characters, or she can go to big people's church. But she's going *somewhere.*

I hear you: "Brother Jim, you're a big meanie! Kicking poor little Millie Mae out of a ministry she loves!" Listen, I'm not throwing Millie Mae out of the church. I'm not telling her she can't work in children's ministry. I appreciate her thirty years of faithful service. But I need to align her with a job that fits her abilities and gifts. She's the wrong person for the job she's in.

If Millie Mae is primarily motivated to serve God and serve kids, she'll willingly go where she fits best. Or she'll grow in her abilities so she fits where she is.

And if she quits in a huff...well, I won't miss her. Huffiness is not a characteristic I want in volunteers anyway. I'll give her a going-away party and wish her well in her new place of service. I'll even help her find a new job that fits, if she'll let me.

But she's not going to keep boring the kids in church.

Take your time getting people placed in your program. You're building a team and discerning giftedness, not just scribbling names onto an organizational chart.

In the *wrong* places...

What determines where you should place a volunteer?

I'll admit it first: Sometimes I've gone looking for someone to fill a slot in my lineup. I need a fourth-grade teacher, so that's where you're going. Maybe you tell me you'd rather work with preschoolers, but I've got a waiting list of teachers for those classrooms so I tell you to think of the fourth-graders as big preschoolers and in you go.

That's not respecting what God's wired you to do.

Sometimes we get the wrong people in a job because we *put* people there. We don't discern where people should go—we just slap them into jobs we need filled. When someone is in the wrong job, they're going to fail. Guaranteed.

Other times people end up in the wrong jobs because they tell us what they'd *like* to do instead of what they *can* do. We're scared of hurting their feelings, so we let those folks push on ahead and fill spots someone else should fill.

Listen, I'd like to sit in the pilot's seat when I fly somewhere too. It's got lots of legroom, a great view, and holds the first person to get to the destination. But I've got no business being there, and American Airlines (I have over a million air miles with them) is smart enough not to offer me the option to book that seat.

At the *wrong* time...

By "wrong time" I don't mean showing up late for a meeting. I mean people volunteering to serve other people's kids when they should be home serving their *own* kids.

I mean a mom who's so busy serving on committees and planning commissions that she's away from home six nights a week.

I mean a dad who's willing to spend hours preparing a lesson for his Sunday morning class but is too busy to do any Bible reading with his own children.

I mean parents who have a chronically ill child or a parent in declining health.

I mean Christians whose spiritual lives are suffering because they've been making some poor discipleship choices and are in no condition to counsel others about how to grow in faith.

There are seasons in life, and during some of those seasons it's smart to step away from volunteering. If there's too little time, energy, or stability in a volunteer's life for that person to do a good job, it's better if the volunteer sits on the sidelines for a spell while fixing what's broken.

Back when I played high school football, we used to be *proud* when we played injured. When I sprained a finger or twisted an ankle, I'd just grit my teeth and play through the pain—because that's what manly football players did. They didn't let a little thing like a ripped-off ear or an exploded kidney or a separated shoulder keep them on the bench.

Boy, was I stupid back then.

When you play injured you do two foolish things at the same time: You don't give your body a chance to heal, and you hurt your team's chances of winning.

Forget what you're doing to yourself—think about your team. You're out there on the field looking like you've got what it takes to perform your best—and you don't. You're hobbling around while there's a perfectly good substitute sitting on the bench, just waiting to get called into the game.

There are times it's not smart for people to volunteer in the children's ministry program. Don't ask people to play through their pain—it won't work out for them, your kids, or you. Let them heal, then bring them back into the game.

For the *wrong* reasons...

There are lots of reasons someone might volunteer to serve in children's ministry, and most of them are OK...*if* the primary reason is to serve God and kids.

Maybe someone wants to gain a little teaching experience. To build a resume. To work alongside friends. That's all good, as long as the primary focus is on what God is doing in the lives of children.

Of course, some reasons are *never* OK:

- The volunteer has a desire to damage children in any way, shape, or form.
- Because the volunteer is bored and has nothing better to do.
- Because the volunteer is avoiding dealing with someone or something else, and the nursery is a good place to hide out while at church.

Any of those reasons—and some others—will keep you out of my children's ministry. You might be able to do the job, but you won't be doing it for the right reasons, and that'll eventually show. Without the right motivation, a volunteer creates *way* more problems than he or she solves.

As far as motivating volunteers goes, the fundamental truth is this: *You can't do it.* What motivates your volunteers was wired into them way before they came to see you. All you can do is help deliver the benefits your volunteers want to realize as a result of participating in children's ministry.

I've thought a lot about what motivates volunteers and what different kinds of volunteers want from volunteering. When it gets down to the basics, I think there are three kinds of volunteers: foremen, roofers, and building inspectors.

Stick with me while I explain.

First, you've got to understand that there's a fair amount of new construction in Tulsa, and now and then it's fun for me to watch a house go up. It happens almost overnight sometimes— whole new subdivisions shooting up in the middle of what was a horse pasture the month before.

There are three kinds of people who show up at each construction site: foremen, roofers, and building inspectors. They remind me a lot of the volunteers who show up at my children's ministry.

Foremen

Foremen *love* seeing results.

These are the guys with the blueprints and construction schedules. They set goals, solve problems, and know where they're going.

Foremen tend to be organized, be comfortable with deadlines, and have a "to-do" list that's prioritized and plugged into two pocket organizers and a spreadsheet. Foremen like to take on sizable challenges that mean something.

You've got foremen as volunteers, too. They're the organized ones even if they're not the ones in charge.

The thing is, if they're not in charge and *nobody's* in charge, they get frustrated. They'll step up to the plate if only because it drives them nuts that time's being wasted.

If you want to motivate a foreman: Hand him or her a plaque, testimonial, or other tangible award to hang on the wall. A promotion to an even more responsible job matters, too.

If you want to encourage foremen to stick long term: Arrange for them to be responsible for an entire, defined area of ministry. Give them the chance to set and meet goals and "do things right."

Roofers

I don't know what it is with roofers, but around here they never work alone. If there's one roofer nailing down shingles, there are at least half a dozen roofers. And they seem to enjoy talking with one another at least as much as they enjoy the work.

Roofers are people who love to interact with others. They care about the interaction about as much as they care about the work.

The roofers at your church don't carry nail guns, but you can still spot them: They're the ones walking up to visitors and greeting those folks. They love being part of your church community, and relationships are hugely important to roofers. They're good listeners and enthusiastic presenters.

There's a downside: Because they're caring, nurturing, and sensitive, they tend to get their feelings hurt easily. You've got to move slowly with roofers and give them time to debrief their feelings.

If you want to motivate a roofer: Take time to establish a relationship, and send a personal note. Throw a barbecue or potluck, and let the roofer hang out with friends.

If you want to encourage roofers to stick long term: Provide opportunities for meeting new friends and maintaining existing friendships. Provide personalized training and touch-bases.

Building Inspectors

These people care about power. On a construction site they're the ones who decide if the plumbing is up to code—or not. They determine if the electric wires are OK as is or need to be torn out and reinstalled. They care about influence and having an impact on outcomes, which isn't necessarily bad—but it *can* be.

If they have a healthy win-win view of power, they're great allies. They'll use their influence to bring everyone on board and make everyone successful, then they'll stand in the corner beaming as a project comes together.

But if they're the type of building inspectors who like to throw their weight around and hold a win-lose view of power, it's a disaster. They make pronouncements, value being "right" over being righteous, and generally mow down anyone in their way—you included.

If you want to motivate a building inspector: Recognize the person in front of peers, or give the person a letter of commendation. It'll end up framed and on a study wall.

If you want to encourage building inspectors to stick long term: Let the person teach a class, lead a meeting, or assume another position of influence. Give the person a title and a chance to serve as a ministry liaison with a larger group. But be careful: Be sure the power isn't misused.

Only God can rewire what motivates people at a foundational level, but there *is* something that happens as volunteers stick with a ministry awhile: Their motivation shifts from external to internal, from extrinsic to intrinsic.

Often people become volunteers because someone they like or respect asks them to get involved. They sign up to make Jack happy or because Jody needs help.

Or they sign on because they want to be involved in their children's lives—when their kids are in elementary school, that's where they serve. Or maybe they got swayed by a great sales pitch from the pulpit and signed up before they realized what they were doing.

All those are fair reasons—and they're all extrinsic.

But before long, people see they're making a difference. They're having an impact on kids' lives. At some point they decide to stick around even if Jack quits or Jody leaves the church. Or when their kids move on to the high school department. They're intrinsically motivated—and they're totally on board.

NEXT STEPS—THE NUTS AND BOLTS

So how do you get there?

Let's tackle the challenges one at a time.

In the next chapter we'll explore how to get the right people—volunteers who have the right skill and gift mix and are excited about serving. To do that you've got to get people signed up. I'll tell you how we've been able to get more than 1,100 volunteers working in my children's ministry.

Most churches rank "getting volunteers" as one of the challenges they face. Forget recruiting the *right* volunteers; they're just looking for warm bodies that haven't been arrested lately.

That's not good enough for the kids I serve. They deserve better. So if someone's going to volunteer at Church On The Move, that person is going to jump through some hoops. I want to know what volunteers expect from me, and they need to know what I expect from them—before they get into a volunteer job. It's a two-way street.

But I won't find great volunteers until I get lots of folks looking to sign up for children's ministry. Once I've got more people than I absolutely need, then I can afford to be picky.

And I *want* to be picky. I *want* to pick and choose. I'm like that woman at the supermarket who squeezes every apple on the table before she picks the three she's taking home. She wants the best and she's patient enough to get it.

In Chapter 5 we'll talk about recruitment—how to get yourself a big batch of potential volunteers. Your "right people" are in that group. I'll show you how to get people by looking at how Jesus got people. Then, in Chapters 6 and 7, we'll talk about getting those right people into the right jobs. There's a process that encourages that to happen and helps you create volunteers who stick. It takes a little work, but it isn't hard. I'll walk you through the steps to get it done.

My goal is to get you fully stocked with great volunteers, because until you've got them in place you can't move ahead and do the things that will *keep* them there...*keep* them growing...and turn them into volunteers who *stick*.

But first things first.

Let's get some folks signed up.

chapter 5

Recruiting
Like Jesus Recruited

You can't get volunteers to stick with your program until you get
volunteers in the first place. Here's how Jesus got people—you can
use the same techniques and get all the great people you need.

Whenever I ask a conference audience if they have
questions, I always hear "Brother Jim, how do you recruit volunteers?"

One reason I get that question is that at my church we have
lots of children's ministry volunteers. And I mean *lots*—we've
got just over 1,100 different positions filled.

Plus we've got a *waiting* list to work in some areas.

You might shake your head and wonder if we're paying people...threatening people...or if there's something in the water
here in Tulsa. Not everyone who comes to our church plugs in as
a volunteer, but a whole lot of them do.

What *is* it with our people?

It's this: *Our church* expects *church members to volunteer in a
ministry*. We expect it, and our church leaders talk about it and
model it.

We don't apologize for that expectation because it doesn't
come from us—it comes from the Lord. He expects people to use
what he's given them in ministry. He expects stewardship not
just of money but of time and abilities as well.

If you're bashful about expecting people to volunteer, no

wonder you've got a volunteer shortage. If your leadership doesn't model volunteering, no wonder nobody takes you seriously when you ask for volunteers.

If you're going to recruit like Jesus recruited, you'd better get over being bashful or apologetic. He took involvement *very* seriously. With Jesus you were either in the game or you weren't; there wasn't room for a cheering section that never actually got out of the stands.

One reason we have so many volunteers who stick is that we take them and their involvement seriously. We ask for and get a significant commitment. From the very get-go they know they're signing up for something that matters.

We stole that approach from Jesus, but he doesn't seem to mind.

The results speak for themselves. I've got some of the finest volunteers I've ever met serving with me, and I'd trust them with my life. Even more—I've trusted them with my *children's* lives as my daughters have grown up in those classrooms.

I want to introduce you to Jesus' recruitment principles and practices and tell you how we've put them to use.

The Recruitment Principles and Practices of Jesus

Jesus had a lot to say about recruiting volunteers.

People always seem surprised to hear that. We've come to believe that "recruitment" was invented about the time the bulletin board was unveiled. I mean, how could anyone recruit before there were bulletin boards? Where did Jesus post sign-up sheets?

Jesus recruited people without bulletin boards. Without bulletin inserts. Without pulpit announcements. Somehow, he was able to recruit people as "disciples," which involved more than a six-month commitment and a training meeting.

Listen to Jesus as he describes what life would be like if you followed him:

"I have come to bring fire on the earth, and how I wish it were already kindled! But I have a baptism to undergo, and how distressed I am until it is completed! Do you think I came to bring peace on earth? No, I tell you, but division. From now on there will be five in one family divided against each other, three against two and two against three. They will be divided, father against son and son against father, mother against daughter and daughter against mother, mother-in-law against daughter-in-law and daughter-in-law against mother-in-law" (Luke 12:49-53).

Try using *that* speech to sign up your VBS workers. See how far you get.

My point: Jesus never soft-pedaled what it would be like to volunteer in his traveling ministry. It was always a life-changing, lifelong commitment. And *still* he managed to sign people up to do more than run the snack table.

That's why Jesus is my model for recruiting volunteers. I think he showed us everything we need to know about it in his ministry.

See for yourself. Here are fifteen recruitment principles and practices Jesus used in his ministry on earth that we've adopted with great success.

1. Jesus demonstrated enthusiasm.

Do you think it made a difference that Jesus was enthusiastic about the kingdom of God? That when he talked about serving God he could point to himself as an example?

Those things surely mattered.

People want to see that their leader is fired up—and practicing what he or she preaches.

Write this in the margin: *Your best children's ministry recruiter is your pastor.* Until you have your pastor's enthusiastic support, you're pretty much talking to yourself.

Your pastor is the one who can help establish a culture where service is expected—a culture that opens the floodgates of people who want to find a place to plug in. At Church On The Move, our pastor communicates in a hundred ways that working with kids is important. He builds esteem for what we do and actively supports us. I simply couldn't be successful without his help.

Your pastor is the one who can communicate to the entire church that children's ministry is important. Who can recognize your children's workers some Sunday morning and let them bask in well-deserved applause. Who can stop by your staff meeting to say a few words of thanks to your teachers.

Until your pastor appreciates what you're doing, don't expect many other people to appreciate it. So if your pastor isn't a children's ministry fan, make an effort to get your pastor on board. Schedule appointments to keep the pastor updated on what you're doing and what results you're seeing. Stay on the radar screen through e-mails, staff meetings, or casual conversations.

Your best children's ministry recruiter is your pastor. Remember that.

2. Jesus recruited by vision.

Nobody wants to help you if you're pitiful and your program is broken. Why should they? Maybe the program isn't worth doing, or you're a lousy leader. Either way, they'll steer clear of you.

So don't talk about your desperate need for volunteers. Talk about what people selected to serve in children's ministry do and the impact they have on young lives.

If you're leading your children's ministry, *you are the vision-caster.* It's your job to communicate the significance of children's ministry in your church. Share that vision with passion. With power. With poise. Talk about it constantly—it's what you're calling people to.

Jesus talked about the kingdom of God, and people responded. Could they see it? Taste it? Touch it? Not really...but they could *feel* it. They felt it in the words of Jesus and the vision he shared. The kingdom of God was at hand—that's something to get excited about!

What *is* your children's ministry vision statement? What's your mission statement? What exactly are you trying to accomplish? You *must* have vision and mission statements. Without them, you've got nothing to say to potential volunteers. Why should they care about working with you if you can't explain the purpose of your ministry?

Once you have a vision statement, talk it up. Talk it *way* up, and get excited while you're doing it. Your vision will attract like-minded people to your ministry because they'll get excited about the same things that excite you.

How to Write a Vision Statement

A vision statement is a description of what a perfect future would look like. It sets your direction.

For instance, your vision statement might say, "Our children's ministry will serve and glorify God by encouraging the Christian growth of children."

Pretty simple, but it tells people what you're about. You want kids to grow spiritually and in things of the Lord. So if people don't like kids, or they aren't interested in spiritual growth, maybe they'd better skip signing up to help you.

A few things to keep in mind:

Make sure your children's ministry vision statement lines up with your church's overall vision. Your job is to serve the larger vision, not set off in your own direction.

Get people involved who have an interest. Put together a committee with your pastor, some parents, some children's ministry leaders, and any other people who have a vested interest. Work together so nobody gets surprised. Plus people are more likely to support a vision statement if they've had a part in creating it.

Keep it simple. You're defining the big idea that will guide your decisions and keep you on track. Don't get into details.

And if you can't get excited about a vision and mission that involve helping children get to know Jesus, then ask somebody to check your pulse. You may need to be resuscitated.

I've included a method for developing both vision and mission statements. Don't skip developing them! They bring power and purpose to your recruitment efforts!

3. Jesus walked the talk.

Have you ever seen ads for gyms? They always show people with perfect abs working out. And they're *smiling* while they work out. They can't think of anything they'd rather do than twelve thousand deep knee bends.

But when you go to those gyms, you know what you see? People who look like me. People who've got some sag issues. We're the "before" pictures the gym didn't show you.

The only people who look perfect are the instructors.

Good thing, too. I wouldn't sign up to learn how to get in shape from someone who looked like me. Mercy—that takes "the blind leading the blind" to a whole new level.

It's like that with ministry, too. If you want to get folks signed up to work in children's ministry, have a heart for it yourself. If you want leaders who have a relationship with Jesus, have one yourself. If you want prayer warriors, you be a prayer warrior.

Whatever I require others to do, I have to do, too. Volunteers value authenticity. They value integrity. Have both.

Jesus is the ultimate example of that. He didn't expect James and John to walk away from the family business to serve God without doing the same thing himself. Jesus was faithful all the way to the cross. He has the moral authority to ask the same of you.

When you're asking people to volunteer in service, you'd better be doing the same thing yourself.

HOW TO WRITE A MISSION STATEMENT

A *mission statement tells folks what you want to do—your purpose. It answers the question, "Why do we exist?"*

Let's say your mission statement is "We will present the gospel to children and help them know, love, and follow Jesus."

You're about sharing your faith. You may set up an after-school program, a Sunday school, and a baseball camp, but the top priority of all of those things will be the presentation of the gospel and discipleship.

A few things that have to happen as you develop a mission statement:

Get buy-in from all the interested groups. *That might include parents, your pastor, a Sunday school teacher, and kids. Again—get them on board now and you'll have fewer objections later.*

Make sure your mission statement lines up with your vision statement. *It's the "why" to your vision statement's "what."*

Keep it simple. *If it uses big words or runs on for half a page, it won't communicate what you're trying to do or keep everyone focused. It'll be one more page nobody reads in the volunteer handbook.*

4. Jesus made everything a matter of prayer— including recruitment.

Forty days in the wilderness. Forty days of prayer and fasting. Jesus had plenty of time to talk things through with God.

It's not recorded what Jesus prayed about, but I believe with all my heart that he asked God to lead him to the right people. I believe that because the first thing Jesus did when he walked out of the wilderness was recruit.

You and I have a tendency to do everything *but* pray. When it looks like we'll be eight ushers short for the children's choir concert next Saturday, we burn up those phone lines begging for help. We usually forget to stop, put down the phone, and talk things over with God.

God already knows you need eight ushers. Or maybe he knows not many people will show up for the concert, so you really don't have a problem. If your intent is to cooperate with God's purposes, doesn't it make sense to ask God what they are? Whom he wants standing in the aisles next Saturday to greet and welcome visitors?

Jesus kept the first thing first: He kept his relationship with his heavenly Father first and foremost, making time to pray. *And* to listen to God. And as a result, he did pretty well in the recruitment department. He got all the people he needed to fulfill prophecy and to establish the church.

We should all do as well.

Are you praying for the Lord to bring you the right people to staff your children's ministry?

5. Jesus took his time to fill the roster.

Jesus needed twelve disciples...but he recruited in ones and twos. Could Jesus have lined up twelve recruits faster? I think so—but he wouldn't have gotten the people he wanted.

Something to remember: "A bird in the hand is worth two in the bush" is *not* a biblical proverb.

We recruit that way, though. When the pastor tells us a second (or third) service will be added and to ramp up the nursery staff, we're tempted to grab any warm body willing to volunteer. We want to get those slots on the organizational chart filled *now*.

That's not how Jesus operated, and you'd better not operate that way, either. You'll end up with people who aren't the people you need. They won't be happy, and they won't stick.

6. Jesus instituted a draft.

Jesus wasn't shy about getting the people he wanted on his team. In fact, he didn't recruit them as much as he drafted them.

"You come and follow me" doesn't sound like a question. It's a command.

I don't have quite the authority Jesus has, but when it comes to getting people working in children's ministry, I don't ask for volunteers either.

Here's my favorite way to recruit people: I walk up to folks in my church and ask, "What are you doing in this church?" Most of the time they say, "Nothing."

So I say, "That's what I thought. Fill out this four-page worker application. I'm going to make a children's worker out of you."

And you know what I hear? Usually I hear, "OK."

That means I'm always looking to connect with people who have gotten into the church but haven't found a place to do ministry. They hear that they're supposed to, but they're kind of vague on what that means and where to start.

Buddy, I *fix* that problem for them.

I was at Sam's Club one day loading up on stuff we needed for a big kids' event. I was paying with a personal check and the checkout lady asked for my place of employment as she was scribbling information down on the back of my check.

"Church On The Move," I said, and that's the first time she really stopped to look at me.

"Oh, you're Brother Jim," she said, smiling.

"That's right," I replied. "How are you? *Who* are you? Do you go to our church?"

And this lady said, "Oh, yes." She'd just finished up our membership class.

"Are you doing anything in ministry yet?" I asked.

She said she wasn't.

"Then why aren't you working in children's ministry?"

You know what she said? She said, "Well, I want to work with preschoolers, but I don't know how."

She was looking at the right guy to help her with *that*. Since she was going on break in a few minutes, I asked if I could buy her a cup of coffee in the little snack shop they've got there. She could fill out one of the four-page worker applications I always carry with me in the car, and I'd take it back to the preschool director.

She thought that would be just fine.

"Listen," I said, "Does anybody else from our church work here?"

Three other church ladies were also working, so I asked if she'd round them up. I'd buy them coffee, too.

When I got back to the church, I walked over to my preschool director and handed her those completed applications. "Where'd you get *these*?" she asked.

"Sam's," I said. "They've got *everything* you need for ministry."

Back when my girls were little, I planned daddy-daughter dates during women's fellowship meetings. Julie brought the girls to meet me in the lobby of the women's ministry area, and while I was waiting I stood around making eye contact. The fact my daughters were coming kept the women from deciding I was a stalker and calling the police.

Women would see me and ask what I was doing there. "Just waiting on my girls," I'd answer. "Say, what are you doing in the church? You love babies, don't you? Why don't you work in the nursery?"

While I was waiting on my girls, I could recruit twelve, fifteen folks.

I was astounded at how often people would thank me for approaching them about volunteering. They'd say, "I was just waiting for somebody to ask me."

And I'm thinking, *Didn't you see the bulletin inserts? Didn't you hear the announcements? We've been talking about this for months!*

But they wanted to be asked, face to face. I understand that because I'm the same way: I want to be wanted. There's nothing like personal contact and a direct question.

And where did I learn that? By watching Jesus.

Toward the end of Jesus' earthly ministry, he was talking to his disciples and he said, "You did not choose me, but I chose you to go and bear fruit—fruit that will last" (John 15:16a). Those are the words of someone who drafted help.

Now keep in mind that when I ask people to work in the nursery, I'm asking them to *apply* to work in the nursery. I'm inviting them to enter into a discussion about whether they're the right people to work in the nursery. They won't necessarily end up working with babies; we'll sort that out through the interview process.

But until we get talking, nothing happens.

7. Jesus seized opportunities.

Those women got it wrong: I *am* a stalker. I'm always stalking volunteers. I'm a faithful husband and not a day goes that I don't thank God for the wonderful, attractive woman he gave me to be my wife. Julie, if you're reading this, know that when I said, "Till death do us part," I meant it.

But there *are* women who turn my head. You march a woman down the hall in our church building and I see her smile at kids she passes—that's a woman I want to meet. I want to give her a worker application and challenge her to take that warmth toward kids and put it to good use in a classroom. I want her name, phone number, and address. I'll pass that information along to the woman who runs our preschool Sunday school program.

Julie's gotten used to this. It comes with the territory, because I've noticed that Jesus went out *looking* for volunteers. He didn't wait for volunteers to come find him.

When Jesus recruited his first disciples, he was walking out by the Sea of Galilee—he wasn't back in his office behind a desk filling out paperwork. He was out drafting the people he needed.

Here's my advice for any children's ministry leader who's frustrated with not having enough help: *Go out and find people.* Go where people are. I go to church, to men's meetings, to women's meetings...anywhere I might find people who love God and who haven't found a place to plug into service yet.

And I'll run databases from the church computer too. I run a list of all our members, then a list of people who are already volunteering somewhere else. That gives me a list of potential volunteers.

I'm always looking, and guess what? That means I'm always finding, too.

8. Jesus talked about rewards.

I know: Rewards are supposed to be a bad thing. We want kids to be intrinsically motivated, not extrinsically motivated. And I'd rather have a volunteer show up because she loves Jesus than because she's forming relationships so she can expand her interior decorating business.

But Jesus talked about rewards. He told people about heaven.

He reminded them that he was the way, the truth, and the life, and that nobody got to heaven except through him. That's a powerful incentive to follow Jesus.

And the fact is there *are* rewards that come with giving oneself to service as a volunteer. Those rewards are natural outcomes of volunteering. Why not talk about them? They're there.

I've already shared a bit about connecting with volunteers' motivations and how motivations can shift from extrinsic to intrinsic. But in every step of their careers, volunteers want to know they're making a difference. They want to do something important. And, truth be told, they're looking to get something out of the experience.

Jesus talked about all of that. He talked about rewards (read Matthew 5:1-12, for starters). He talked about our motivations (Matthew 5:21-24). And Jesus told Peter and Andrew, "I will make you fishers of men." Peter knew Jesus was going to make something out of him, that Jesus would do something significant with him.

Don't be afraid to talk about what's in it for your volunteers. It's better to be clear about that and set realistic expectations.

9. Jesus required commitment, not just sacrifice.

Jesus didn't make it easy for people who were coming to help him. Read through the Gospels with a highlighter, and mark everything Jesus had to say about volunteering. Jesus never once asked someone to sacrifice. Instead, he asked for commitment. The sacrifices followed, but they flowed out of a decision to be a faithful follower—so they weren't really sacrifices at all. They were simply the cost of discipleship.

Some of the things Jesus asked people to do were specific to those people. For instance, I don't have to give up my fishing business to follow Jesus. That was what Jesus asked of James and John, not Jim Wideman.

But the level of commitment is the same. I have to put God before my work. I may not have to physically leave my family behind to walk from town to town like the twelve disciples, but I *do* have to put God first. I've got to be willing to pack it up and go elsewhere if God tells me to do that.

You see, Jesus required commitment. He didn't waver on

that. If people wouldn't commit, they couldn't follow.

When I'm recruiting volunteers, I ask for commitment, too. There was a time I'd say, "Look, I just want you to cover this week." Or I might get my courage up and say, "I need you to take the whole quarter—could you find it in your heart to do that?"

No more, buddy. God blessed the little things people were doing, but it was frustrating. We were constantly scrambling for volunteers. Plus the quality of leadership that kids experienced was all over the map. There wasn't constancy.

So we said, "No more once-a-monthers. The minimum requirement to work in the Christian education department is serving two times a month." There were some people that quit, but there were far more folks who said, "I'll step up and do that."

We took off and grew to another level. I had the *best* workers I'd ever had. A couple of years later, I said, "It's time to grow. We're going to step up again. I want everybody to commit to working three weeks on and one week off."

Some folks hollered. Some folks moaned. Some of those folks didn't make the cut, but the ones who did—and all the volunteers who came after that—they're the best workers I ever had in my *life*. We still have that commitment level in our preschool, but in the elementary level volunteers work six weeks and then take one week off.

And those volunteers? They're the best staff in the world.

I know that cultural trends would say to make every volunteer job something people can do without having to commit much time and effort. And I could do that—but I won't. Our kids deserve better. They need the consistency, and the volunteers need the time to get better at what they do. If I put you in a job and let you do it once a month for an hour—how long before you think you'd get good at it? A *long* time, that's how long.

If you're someone in my church who has kid contact—you're a teacher or bus ministry captain or children's worship leader—you know what's going on from week to week. You know what's happening in the lives of the children. You're building relationships with kids. You're on top of things because you're there.

I don't want to give that up. And you know what? Neither do our volunteers.

A few months ago I gave out awards to church volunteers

who've been with us for five and ten years. I loved that. I loved seeing people who stepped up to the standards we have for children's ministry here. These are people we've asked to do a lot—and they've come through.

And here's what's best: After a few months, someone may have a job down cold—but they discover they don't have your heart for ministry. They haven't been around long enough to be influenced by the ministry's vision and mission.

I ask volunteers for only a six-month commitment because I know that in six months they'll be successful in their jobs. And the time commitment won't scare them off.

But believe me: I'll use every minute in those six months to instill a deep passion for ministry in those volunteers. If I can get the right heart in those folks, they'll never quit. The six months they've committed is just the introduction.

10. Jesus went after good people.

The people Jesus recruited were busy, hardworking people. I've heard it said, "Well, those disciples were just old fishermen. They had plenty of time on their hands."

Wrong. They were small-business owners. People with families. People with obligations. People who had enough to do without adding Jesus to their lives. They were...well, they were a lot like folks in your church.

Listen, it's just smart to look for volunteers from among the ranks of people who have already figured out how to do two or three things at once. If you want people who can manage a classroom or a department, look for people who are managers at work. If you want people who can handle discipline issues over in junior church, see if any of your church members work with challenging kids during the week.

I've got CEOs volunteering for me. They know how to put together a budget when we're doing a new project. I've got people with commercial art degrees who showed up to decorate our nursery and preschool rooms, and those rooms are beautiful. I've got mechanics, carpenters, and people who can do almost anything we need to have done.

And here's what's great: *They're being trained by their workplaces to be better at what they do here at church.* Every time one of our volunteers attends a safety class at work, that's training she'll put to use here at church, too—and it didn't cost us a cent.

Should you recruit only people who are working and who are doing well in their jobs? Of course not. You're looking for people God has equipped to be effective in ministry, not necessarily people who have mastered their daily jobs.

But I'll be honest: There's a correlation there. People who are reliable and sharp, who can do the things that get them noticed at work—they're the kind of people who are reliable and sharp in children's ministry, too. They show up on time. They do what they say they'll do.

Many of your long-term volunteers will be people who are handling significant responsibilities during the week. It may be running a multimillion-dollar company, or it may be getting four kids up and to school on time. I figure those two jobs take about the same amount of managerial expertise.

Do *not* be shy about recruiting people who are already busy. God's gifted them, you need them, go ask them.

11. Jesus let his volunteers do recruiting.

Jesus was creating the most significant organization in the world: the church. He was putting the cornerstones of that institution in place, collecting the disciples to whom he'd delegate sharing the gospel with the world.

And he didn't even go pick out all twelve of the disciples himself.

Jesus let his early disciples do some recruiting, too. Read John 1:35-51. It was Andrew who went and fetched Peter. And Philip went off and brought back Nathanael.

Now, if Jesus could trust somebody else to pick the Twelve, why can't you encourage your folks to also do recruiting?

You can—and you should.

Here's what I do: I go to the people who are solid, steady, long-term volunteers, people I wish I could clone. I tell them what I appreciate about them. I describe exactly what they do that makes them so successful. Then I ask them to find me a couple more people just like them.

And lots of times, they do!

See, people tend to hang out with people who share their

values. When my mama said, "Birds of a feather flock together," she was warning me to quit hanging out with the dope-smoking, class-cutting crowd, but she was also stating a very important volunteer recruitment principle.

Who are your top volunteers? Have you given them permission to rustle up some new volunteers? Do they know what you're looking for?

Jesus trusted his people. You can do the same.

Shannon Orr is a master teacher in one of our classes for five-year-olds, and she's a great one for spotting good people for children's ministry. The people she picks take to working with children like ducks to water. Here's her secret...

"I look for parents of great kids," she says. "If there's a great kid there's probably a great parent there too. And those parents are honored to help when they're asked. You can tell who wants to take time for kids because they're taking time for their own children."

Preach it, sister!

12. Jesus demonstrated how to do ministry.

Jesus' disciples didn't know it, but when they watched him preach, teach, and heal, he was grooming them to do the same. Jesus knew what they'd be called on to do in a few short years, so he modeled ministry for them.

If you're just *telling* people how to do their jobs instead of actually *showing* them, you'll have three problems:

• *Quality will suffer.*

I'm happy to report I haven't had to go through surgery often. But when I have, I don't ask if the surgeon has read a book about the operation I'm getting. I don't ask if they covered that surgery in medical school.

I want to know how many times the surgeon has done that operation, and I'm hoping to hear a big number. Why? Because there's no substitute for experience, and practice makes perfect.

• *People will be confused.*

You may think you were perfectly clear when you said, "Discipline needs to be redemptive, not punitive." Nobody raised a hand when you asked if there were questions.

But you've still got problems.

Mrs. Smith interpreted that to mean she's not allowed to do anything that might somehow be taken as punishment. That's why there are kids hanging off the overhead fluorescent lights in her classroom.

Mr. Jones figured you meant it's best to nip discipline problems in the bud, so he's got half his kids in detention and the other half doing push-ups.

And Ms. Trujillo isn't sure what you meant, but she knows she doesn't want to work for someone who can't explain how to handle discipline. She up and quit.

When you explain, things can be fuzzy. When you demonstrate, they're clear. *You must model what you want done.* Anything less isn't really training…and it's going to frustrate your volunteers.

• *People will think they're trained when they're not.*

I do some target shooting, and you know who the most dangerous person is on a firing range? It's not the guy shooting for the first time. He's so afraid he'll hurt himself or someone else that he takes every step slow and easy.

And it's not the woman who's been shooting for ten years and can pick a fly off the top of the target. She's developed habits that keep her—and everyone else—safe.

It's the guy who's been shooting three or four times and thinks he knows it all. That some of the safety rules are optional. That nothing's going to go wrong since nothing's gone wrong yet. *That's* the guy who'll be explaining to an emergency room doctor how he managed to shoot off his big toe.

A little bit of knowledge is a dangerous thing. That's true on a shooting range, and it's true in a classroom.

When you've only heard how to handle a classroom situation—that's a little bit of knowledge. When you've seen it done and talked about it afterward, that's enough knowledge to keep your big toes safe.

13. Jesus coached and corrected volunteers.

Maybe this seems more like training than recruiting, but I think it's a powerful recruiting tool to let folks know they can expect input about how they're doing. People want to do well. They don't want to be tossed to the kindergartners and told to fend for themselves.

Peter discovered Jesus wasn't shy about giving feedback, and so did the rest of the disciples. But notice this: The Twelve weren't corrected in front of a larger group. Jesus always seems to have pulled aside the person or persons who needed a talking to and did it privately.

I like that approach, and I've adopted it. I don't correct a teacher or leader when there are kids or peers around. I wait until later and then do my coaching. It cuts down on defensiveness and makes for better learning.

When you're recruiting, be very clear that there will be evaluations. It won't chase off potential volunteers, and it'll encourage some of them.

14. Jesus expected results.

Jesus expected his followers to bear fruit. Read Matthew 7:16-23 and you'll have a whole new appreciation for the saying, "We don't want any dead wood around here."

I don't think it's unrealistic for volunteers to be growing spiritually. It makes sense that if they're planted where God wants them, and they're relying on God, they'll grow. In fact, if their volunteer work is in any way *hindering* their spiritual growth, that's cause to give them a leave of absence as together you sort out the problem.

What results do you want to see in your volunteers' ministries? In their own lives? Have you spelled those expectations out?

15. Jesus entered into a relationship with his volunteers.

If you've got more than ten or fifteen volunteers, you can't do this alone. Lord knows with 1,100 volunteers I don't know what's happening in the lives of everyone who serves with me.

But we've got a system in place where every volunteer has a supervisor, and it's that supervisor's job to be in a relationship with every volunteer who reports to him or her. You need a system like that too.

Jesus spent time with his team. If you want to recruit and retain the dream team you've always wanted, you can't neglect your volunteers once you've gotten them to sign on the dotted line.

Maybe you're thinking, "I don't have time to meet with everybody. I'm running a ministry here." Fine—but you can make sure *someone* has time to meet with every volunteer. Jesus was never too busy to answer Peter's questions. He wasn't too busy to take his team aside and explain some of the parables that went unexplained to everyone else.

Jesus had a ministry to the masses, but he also had a commitment to his disciples. He didn't just talk to them about their preaching skills. He also talked with them about attitude and motivation, about servanthood and ambition. He taught them to pray. When they walked with Jesus, every topic was fair game. That's because Jesus didn't just want to mold their skills—he also wanted to shape their hearts and minds.

So be available. Consider it part of your job to be intentional about your relationship with the volunteers God calls into your children's ministry.

Keep this in mind about volunteers who stick: At one time each of them was a rookie volunteer. It's your job to get these people—and all your volunteers—planted in the right places, where they can flourish and grow.

That comes with careful placement. In the next chapter I'll tell you where to start in the placement process: Create job descriptions.

cha p t e r **6**

Job Descriptions

Volunteers can't be successful if they're not sure what to do.
Here's how to write job descriptions for your volunteers—and why
it's worth the effort.

Here's something about me you might not know: I collect guitars.

I don't mean "collect" the way people collect souvenir spoons or little glass frogs. I don't just display my guitars—I *play* them.

All twenty-two of them.

You'd think a guy with twenty-two guitars has all the guitars he wants, but that's not the case. I'm always scouting thrift shops, garage sales, and guitar shows looking for a vintage guitar that plays great with a unique sound I haven't heard yet.

A couple times my wife has hinted around about what sort of guitar I might like as a gift. But I don't know—it all depends on how a guitar sounds and how it plays. I can't tell by looking; I've got to pick up the guitar, play it, and hear the sound.

Now how frustrating is that for my wife? She wants to give me a guitar but doesn't know what she's looking for. And I can't tell her. So she's stuck. She wants to do something (buy me a guitar) and do a good job (buy a guitar I actually want), but she doesn't have enough information to be effective.

So being a smart woman, Julie does…nothing.

That *is* the smart thing to do, you know. If she buys a guitar I don't like, she's wasted money. If she keeps hinting, I'll figure out what I'm getting next Christmas. That poor girl is stuck because she doesn't know and she can't ask.

But if you happen to run into Julie, you might mention that George Harrison's custom-made 1968 rosewood Fender Telecaster, the guitar he played in the Beatles' last concert, is up for auction at Bonhams London auction house. They're looking for at least $310,000. If Julie's thinking *Christmas present*, maybe they'll let her pay it off at fifty bucks a month.

She can always ask.

I'll save you doing the math. At $50 per month, with no interest charged, it would take 516 years, 7 months to pay for Harrison's guitar. I'm guessing it won't be under the tree on Christmas morning.

Stuck for Lack of a Job Description

When you want to do a good job and you don't have all the information you need, it's frustrating. You aren't sure what to do, and you're afraid anything you *do* try may be wrong.

Shopping for a spouse is one time you might feel frustrated. Serving as a volunteer at church is another time.

Think about it: If you're asked to be a Sunday school teacher and you're handed a curriculum book, is that enough information? What happens if you don't like one of the lessons—are you allowed to change it? Are you supposed to keep attendance? Are you supposed to lecture, or is it OK to play games?

You don't have all the information you need...and depending on who recruited you and how, you may not have anyone handy to ask.

A job description can go a long way toward eliminating frustration for church volunteers. And spouses, too, come to think of it.

Job descriptions are essential, but you can't *believe* how many churches try to get by without them. Some churches think that because they're small they don't need to go through the trouble of defining jobs.

They're wrong.

Here's what having job descriptions does for your church whether you're big, small, or somewhere in between:

It shows people you've thought things through.

If you want to recruit sharp people, you've got to be a sharp organization. And there's not a sharp, professional person I know who would take a job that didn't have a job description.

When somebody offers you a job and there's no job description, run the other way. If your boss can't tell you what she wants you to do, how will you ever do it well? You can't. You're going to fail for sure.

Listen, if the guy who takes your money when you stop for five minutes to buy milk at the corner store has a job description, why don't the church people who take your kids for two hours each Sunday have one?

It helps you figure out whom you *really* need.

I've heard it called the "halo effect:" When someone is really good at one thing, we assume they're good at other things, too. And while that's the way we think, it's not always the way things are.

Just because Brian is a great teacher doesn't mean he'll make a great camp counselor. Ask him and you're on a fast track to disaster because that boy needs eight hours of sleep or he turns into Godzilla.

Not every volunteer job is the same. They don't all require the same skills or the same amount of time. Some are designed for social people, and others are best filled by folks who love sitting alone in front of a computer.

When you're creating job descriptions, you get a clear look at all those factors. And you develop a sense of whom you're *really* looking for to fill specific jobs. Is it an introvert or extrovert? Someone who likes working with people or with machinery? Someone who'll supervise people or work directly with kids?

Without having a camp counselor job description, you'll think Brian is your go-to guy for camp. And he'll take the job because nowhere is it written down that counselors are on call twenty-four hours a day, and they never get eight hours sleep.

Job descriptions save you from asking the wrong people to take a job. And it saves the wrong people from accepting those jobs.

It gives you something to hand to possible volunteers.

I'll put a volunteer application in your hands in a heartbeat. But if you say, "Brother Jim, I'm interested in working with preschoolers. What sort of jobs do you have there?" then I've got something specific to give you. I can hand you job descriptions for all the volunteer jobs we have in the preschool area. I can tell you what jobs are open. I'm ready to put to work the volunteers I'm praying that God sends me.

Until you've got job descriptions ready, you aren't ready for an outpouring of volunteers. You don't know for sure where you'd use them. You don't know how you'd answer if they asked you, "What job do you have for me?"

It's no wonder God doesn't send more volunteers to some churches. Those churches aren't ready to receive them.

It gives you something to use in interviews.

In the next chapter I'm going to suggest—insist, actually— that you or one of your team interviews each potential volunteer.

If you don't have job descriptions to show that potential volunteer, it's going to be an awkward interview. You'll listen to someone pour out his or her heart and together determine that children's ministry is the right place to serve. And the potential volunteer is going to ask you what jobs you've got open and what it takes to do those jobs well.

And you're going to say, "I'll have to get back to you on that."

Listen, you were about two inches shy of the goal line there. That potential volunteer was ready to become a passionate volunteer. You were about to place someone in exactly the right spot. But you can't because you don't really know all the particulars of each job that's open. You need job descriptions for those roles to have that information at your fingertips.

It gives supervisors something to use in evaluations.

One thing I liked about playing football: You get quick feedback.

When you're a lineman, your job is to keep the guys who wear the other color uniform away from your quarterback. After the ball's snapped, you either hold the line or you don't. You're either on your feet or you're on your back watching some guy run across your chest so he can tackle your quarterback.

Feedback on your performance is no problem because performance standards are clear. Did the quarterback have enough time to run a play or not?

But when you're a children's ministry volunteer, performance standards can get fuzzy. Whose job is it to buy snacks? Whose job is it to pray for kids? Whose job is it to follow up if a child is in the hospital? If you don't tell volunteers in a job description, they won't know.

And if you *do* tell them, you've got to hold volunteers accountable.

Job descriptions let volunteers know what you expect, and supervisors know what to evaluate. Without job descriptions your entire program can slip into hit-or-miss second-best without you knowing it.

That's what job descriptions will do for you—but *not* until you write them and give them to folks.

Now I know you're busy. The idea of working on paperwork doesn't get you excited. Writing job descriptions doesn't sound fun. But it's not hard to write job descriptions. The whole thing is pretty straightforward, and if you do it right—it goes quickly.

"But Brother Jim," you say, "I've already got people working in children's ministry. I can't very well write job descriptions telling them what to do when they're already doing it." Sure you can. You'll just need their help to do it.

Sit down with your current staff one at a time and go through the job description template I've included on page 131. Ask them how they'd fill it in if they were describing what they do. Not what they *think* they should do or think *other* people do, but what *they* actually do.

Here's what you'll find: Sally leads her class differently than Bill leads his class. And I'm not talking about individual styles. I'm talking about goals and the scope of their jobs. Bill may be a "show up and teach" teacher while Sally gives it her all, calling kids on their birthdays and keeping track of whose dog just died.

Yet they're both teachers. And they both think they're doing what's expected of them.

Once you talk with your existing staff, it's up to you to sort out performance standards. But whatever you expect of your volunteers, state it clearly. If you don't tell Bill to call kids on their birthdays, he won't suddenly think of it himself.

YOUR CODE OF CONDUCT

I want to tell you what our basic expectations are of our Christian education workers. These expectations come with every job description—they're foundational. They're a code of conduct.

You may not agree with everything on my list, or you may think it doesn't go far enough. What you put in your code of conduct is between you, God, and your church lawyer. I mention the lawyer because when you set expectations and ask questions about lifestyle issues you're treading on some thin ice. The law has a *lot* to say about that, and laws are different in different places.

Some legal folks say not to put any lifestyle questions in your job description at all; stick them all in a written code of conduct and simply talk about it at your interview. See what your lawyer says in your area—and do it.

Here's what we expect…

1. Every volunteer must be in agreement with our church's tenets of faith. I don't want to find out that someone is confusing kids with theology that contradicts what we as a church understand to be God's truth.

2. People must be members of our church and have attended for at least six months before volunteering. I want to know that volunteers have really committed themselves to our church and that they're then able to make a commitment to the children's ministry.

3. Volunteers must be willing to make a minimum six-month commitment. It's going to take at least two months to get most volunteers trained and comfortable in their jobs; I don't want to start over just about the time a volunteer gets the hang of things. Plus children need to see the same faces from week to week.

4. Volunteers must complete a Helps Ministry Worker Application. This is that four-page application I mentioned earlier. A copy of the form starts on page 135. Use it or adapt it as you see fit. I've removed much of the language that's specific to my church; the general questions remain.

5. Volunteers must be loyal to the pastor and leaders of the church. This is so important. The pastor sets the vision for the church; we don't want a volunteer to be unwilling or unable to follow the pastor's lead. In fact, I expect volunteers to *love* their leaders. Jesus expected his followers to love him, and they did. When you love a leader, going the second mile for that person isn't such a long trip.

6. Volunteers must be faithful to their assigned positions. OK, a volunteer really, *really* wanted to sing solos during the worship time, and instead she's helping with the soundboard. If she's reliable and enthusiastic in serving in her current position, she's far likelier to be invited to do more or to switch jobs later.

7. Volunteers must live a separated Christian life. We set high standards for our Christian education workers. They're role models for our children. We want to know that these adult leaders behave on Friday night the same way they behave on Sunday morning.

At my church we have expectations that include

• no tobacco use,
• no drinking of alcohol, and
• no viewing of pornography.

Those are things we expect. And if you ask around a bit you'll find churches that would add dancing to the list, as well as some pretty specific relationship guidelines.

Again—check with your lawyer. It's worth a phone call.

8. Volunteers must attend all worker's meetings and workshops. We don't hold many, and we don't waste time when we meet, so I expect people to show up. When you sign on to volunteer, that expectation is clearly shared.

9. Volunteers must be faithful in attending regular church services (at least one adult service per week). We want volunteers to be serving out of the overflow in their lives. They need spiritual feeding.

10. Volunteers must give at least three days' notice if they know they'll be absent. I know things come up, and sooner or later every volunteer will miss a scheduled work shift. But we want volunteers to plan ahead and to keep their commitments whenever possible.

11. Volunteers must be at their designated post thirty minutes before services start. Volunteers who show up early aren't stressed when kids walk in. Volunteers who show up early are there when a child is dropped off early. Volunteers who show up early are available to pray for one another and to help out as needed.

12. Volunteers must be neat in their appearance. We don't have a dress code, but we do have standards. Most volunteers catch on when they see their fellow volunteers, but we'll take folks aside and provide feedback if necessary. I want my volunteers to look like people you'd trust with your kids. Feel free to have a "Harleys Forever" tattoo, but cover it up when you're on duty.

13. Volunteers must complete appropriate training courses required in their area of ministry. Training is different for various positions; one size definitely does *not* fit all.

14. Volunteers' home lives must be in order. This doesn't mean they can't ever fight with their spouses or that a registration table volunteer's child can't get sent to detention for cutting classes. It means there can't be serious marital or other problems that will interfere with the volunteer's ability to minister effectively. There are seasons in a volunteer's life when he or she should stay focused solely on what's happening at home.

15. Volunteers must give thirty days' notice when resigning a position. This benefits the ministry, but it also benefits the volunteers. We then have time to plan to release them into the next ministry to which God's calling them and to celebrate what God's doing.

How would your volunteers respond to a list like that?

I've had ministry leaders from other churches tell me that they could never get away with that list. It would eliminate half their current crop of volunteers and scare away everybody else.

So what? Do you really *want* your kids being led by folks who aren't willing to do what's in that list? Not me. Working with children is a high calling, a life-changing ministry. I don't want to trust it to people who aren't serious about the calling or the ministry.

So much for general expectations. You can put those on one code of conduct sheet because everyone who's considering volunteering will get it. Hand it to potential volunteers at their interview and say, "This is what we're expecting from people who serve in this ministry. Is there anything here that raises a concern for you?" Let folks read through your list, then quickly review it with them.

While the code of conduct may be the same for everyone, you'll need to tailor the information on individual job descriptions.

I'm going to walk you through the things you should have on a job description. You could get by with giving less information to your potential volunteers, but I'm a big believer in telling the truth, the whole truth, and nothing but the truth. Lay it all out there where people can see it so they make informed decisions.

JOB TITLE

Are you old enough to remember when the guy who picked up the garbage every Thursday was called the garbage collector? That job title *meant* something because it described what the guy did. If your little brother yelled up at the house, "The garbage collector is here!" you knew who was coming and what he was coming for.

These days that garbage collector has become a "sanitation engineer." A receptionist is the "director of first impressions." The guy who painted my house is a "liquid recoating specialist."

What's up with this? I think it's that everyone likes to feel important. Slapping "engineer" or "architect" or "specialist" on the back end of a title helps folks feel significant.

Well, that's a trend that doesn't need to carry into the church.

When you say you're a worship leader or children's ministry master teacher, that's about as significant as you can get. You're doing ministry. You're shaping hearts and minds for eternity and turning kids toward Jesus. It's the God you serve and the privilege of serving that gives you significance, not your title.

So keep your job titles simple and clear. You don't want someone wasting an hour looking for the "personal sanitation and hygiene materials manipulation expert" when what they really need is a nursery worker to change a diaper.

GOAL OF THE POSITION

People need to know what you want them to *accomplish* not just what you want them to do.

There's an old joke that illustrates this pretty well...

Two old boys were out in the boonies deer hunting, and somehow Ed managed to accidentally shoot Buster. It was a pretty serious thing, and they knew they needed help.

Buster reached into his pocket and pulled out a cell phone. He handed it to Ed. "Here," Buster gasped, "call 911 and they'll tell you what to do." Then Buster lost consciousness.

Ed dialed up the number, got a signal, and in about five seconds he was talking to a 911 operator.

"I accidentally shot Buster and I think he's dead!" Ed shouted into the phone.

The 911 operator was reassuring and told Ed she'd walk him through exactly what Ed needed to do. "The first thing," said the operator, "is to stay calm so you can take action. I can tell you're excited. Take a few deep breaths for me."

Ed did that and sure enough, he could feel his heart quit beating so fast.

"Great," said the operator. "Now, the second thing is to make sure your friend is actually dead."

The operator heard the phone rustle as it was set on the ground. A shot rang out, then Ed came back on the line.

"OK," Ed said. "What's the next thing?"

In this little story (hope you weren't eating breakfast) Ed did really well following directions. He did everything that was asked of him. But because he didn't catch hold of the goal (to save Buster's life), he ended up doing something foolish.

Make sure people understand the goal so they can make good decisions.

WHOM THE VOLUNTEER IS RESPONSIBLE TO, OR REPORTS TO

People change jobs, so don't list a supervisor's name on each job description—list a position instead.

For instance, if I'm a teacher in the fourth grade classroom on Saturday nights, I may report to the master teacher in that classroom. Or I may report to the Sunday school superintendent if that's how my church is organized.

But I report to *someone*. I need to know who's responsible for coaching, challenging, and evaluating me. For seeing that I'm trained, on time, and teaching truth.

Everybody needs a supervisor, because everyone needs accountability and encouragement.

You may think of that as a negative thing—accountability. But it's not. It's a safety net we place under every volunteer at our church. And our volunteers appreciate that.

Charlotte Uzzel has been with us for seven years, and she's as capable a children's ministry volunteer as you could ever hope to have. But part of the reason she's so good is that she's had strong leadership the entire time she's been with us. She's had someone to keep her growing and improving.

And that's just fine with Charlotte.

Her supervisor is actually in the room with her, and her supervisor's supervisor stops in the room each week before class to see if everyone is in place and ready. And to see if anything is needed.

"If there's something we need, all we have to do is say so. The director for our area reviews suggestions and requests weekly—and acts on them.

"And if a teacher is doing something poorly—classroom discipline, for instance—then that person's supervisor will take the teacher aside and coach him or her. If it's a general problem in our area, at our next meeting there will be general coaching given."

No wonder I've got the best volunteers in the world. They're getting ongoing, personalized training and coaching. That wouldn't happen if they were unclear about who their supervisor is or if the supervisors never stopped in.

A Two- or Three-Sentence Summary (or List of Points) Describing the Job

Here's where you sum up what the volunteer will be doing. Go into enough detail so nobody's surprised but not so much detail that you get bogged down.

Be honest on the job descriptions. This isn't a place to sugar-coat the truth. If the nursery assistant is in charge of emptying the diaper pail at the end of the service, say so. If parking lot attendants have to direct traffic whether it's sunny or pouring, make that clear.

By the time people are looking at job descriptions, they've already decided to volunteer. You don't need to sell them on anything. You need to help them make a good choice among the jobs that are available.

The Approximate Time Required per Week or Month

Here's another place to have integrity. Find out from your very best volunteers in each job how long it takes them to prepare and do their jobs.

I get mailings from curriculum publishers that say, "Your teachers can just open up these books and teach—that's how simple these lessons are!" But do you *want* teachers who just expect to open up a book and read? *I* don't. I want teachers who'll pray over their lessons, who'll start on Monday night getting ready for the next Sunday.

People naturally cut corners. They find ways to get things done in less time. But don't you go encouraging that by promising a job takes four hours a month when to do it right really takes fifteen hours.

The "Term" of the Commitment, Stated in Days, Months, or Years

I've mentioned that I expect a six-month commitment from volunteers, and that's true for most of our programming.

But I wouldn't ask for a six-month commitment from vacation Bible school teachers. You probably need those folks for a couple meetings before the event, for the week of the event, and for a wrap-up party when it's over.

And if you've got a need for lots of chair setter-uppers and taker-downers after an event, that can be a one-day commitment. I've got lots of those situations that come up over the course of a year.

Whatever you're expecting, *be clear*. Volunteers need to know when they're able to step down without hearing they've left you high and dry.

Potential volunteers are terrified that if they sign up to teach in the midweek program, they'll be stuck until they die or Jesus comes back, whichever happens first. If they make a commitment for a specific length of time, they relax and enjoy themselves.

And that makes it easier for you to re-recruit them!

A Description of the Training That Will Be Provided

You know what this says? It says you care enough to invest in your volunteers. It says you're not throwing them to the wolves. Even if the training is just quarterly meetings, put it down.

Then do what you promise. The fact that a training session is listed on a job description means the volunteer's supervisor will be checking to see if the volunteer passed the training.

A List of Any Special Qualifications or Unique Skills the Position Requires

If this job requires the volunteer to pass an audition or have a current professional certification, say so.

For instance, you may be the most wonderful, nurturing person on God's green earth, but if you're not a currently certified EMT, nurse, or doctor, I don't want you in the health office at my camp. I need people who are current on those professional credentials, or my insurance company will hunt me down.

In the same way, you might think you're a great drummer, but the music director might have a different opinion. I don't care if you're a professional drummer—you've got to pass an audition to join some of our music teams.

Remember: The first time most volunteers see a job description is during their interview. They *want* to know if there's a credential they need or an audition to pass. They don't want to be surprised with that information down the road.

And something you should know about job descriptions: They aren't Scripture. You can change them without committing heresy.

A time or two I've had a job that was almost a fit with a particular volunteer, but it wasn't quite right. So I changed the job a bit. You're allowed to do that.

Here are some ways to do it:

Supersize the job—add a few tasks so the position is more challenging. Some volunteers who are used to big jobs want a challenge.

Streamline the job—remove some of the menial tasks, or combine tasks so one volunteer has control of more of a complete task.

Diversify the job—avoid a job becoming routine or boring by including things that spice it up. For instance, put the Sunday school teachers in charge of planning the quarterly birthday party for children.

For your convenience, I've included a photocopiable template for you to use as you write job descriptions. It's on page 131. Make a stack of copies and spend time writing, erasing, and rewriting. Sharpen up your descriptions. Then you can type them in for use with your folks.

Plus you'll find a couple of job descriptions I've prepared for our people. Maybe they'll give you some ideas, too. They're on pages 132-134.

Job descriptions are essential for placing the right people in the right volunteer jobs, but there's another step in the placement process: interviewing potential volunteers.

chapter 7

Interviewing and Placement

Here's how to make sure volunteers get into the right jobs—jobs
where they'll fit and they're likely to stick long term.

Some people would rather get a root canal than sit through
an interview. With a root canal they get painkillers and don't
have to answer as many personal questions. Interviews feel like
an invasion of privacy, even if they're not hiding anything. They
just don't want to reveal much about themselves.

So don't expect everyone to be overjoyed when you announce
that interviews are part of getting a volunteer job in your church.
Most people won't mind, but some people will protest.

Let them protest. Stand firm and make it clear that *nobody
gets assigned to a volunteer job until he or she is interviewed.* Period.
No exceptions.

WHY ARE INTERVIEWS SO IMPORTANT?

Interviews are essential for at least six reasons...

1. Interviews let you nudge volunteers in the right direction.

Most people in your church have no idea of all the volunteer
jobs available. They see song leaders, musicians, ushers, and

maybe some people presenting a drama or skit in the sanctuary.

And down in the children's education area they see teachers, registration folks, and supervisors floating around between rooms. They might catch sight of a worship band, too.

But unless they wander the wrong way down the hall, they'll never see volunteers doing administrative work, people counting the offering, or volunteers preparing to do visitation and hospital calls.

Until the full scope of positions is explained during an interview, a potential volunteer will have no idea what all is available.

2. Interviews let you minister to potential volunteers.

Most people do lots of listening at church. They listen to teachers, preachers, announcements, and Easter pageants.

They seldom get to do any talking—especially about themselves.

But that's exactly what happens when we interview new members and volunteers. People talk about who they are, what they like, and what's important to them. And somebody's sitting across from them listening.

You can do a lot of ministry to someone when you're listening. You can hear that person's heart. If someone is volunteering because he's out of a job and needs something to fill his time, or because her husband died and she's lonely, that'll come out in the interview.

When you join Church On The Move, we're going to sit down with you to get to know you. Now, I don't do all those interviews myself. That's all I'd ever *do* if I did every interview personally. We've got a team of people—pastors and lay folks—who handle all those interviews.

But I'll tell you this: I wish I could do all the interviews. If I were in a smaller church I'd save that job for me. Why? Because it's a great place to do ministry.

3. Interviews give you permission to do background screening.

Since 1985, I've caught over three hundred child molesters who have attempted to sign up to work in children's ministry at churches where I've been on staff. One man wanted to work in our nursery, and as a reference he gave me the name of the church where he'd been before coming to us. I called the pastor and heard, "Brother Jim. I'm so glad you called. This guy molested two babies in our nursery."

When I confronted the applicant and told him what I'd heard, he said, "I didn't think you'd really check me out."

We'll check you out, all right. Every person who volunteers for our children's ministry gets a background screening—every one. I ask for references and call them.

Why do convicted child molesters and others who have no business working with children, youth, or other vulnerable people keep signing up for ministry positions? I'll tell you why—because in many churches they have no problem getting those volunteer jobs. Nobody checks their history. Everybody takes their word about where they've been and who they are.

On your applications, *require* people to give their written permission for background screening, which will then be discussed at the interview. When people see you're serious, some will drop out of the volunteer process. And that's fine—you don't want those people on your team.

I know, I know—background screenings are expensive. Depending on the level of screening (just Department of Motor Vehicles? plus criminal history or court actions? just in your area or national?) you'll spend $35 or $40 on up. It can about kill your budget.

Do it anyway. Or if you don't feel you can afford screenings, put up a sign outside each classroom saying, "These leaders haven't been screened by the police. We didn't think we could afford it." See how parents respond.

You can't afford *not* to screen potential volunteers.

4. Interviews let you understand volunteers' motives.

If you don't know what motivates each of your volunteers, it'll cost you. That's because there are a *lot* of motivations for volunteering—and the recognition that satisfies one volunteer won't satisfy another one.

When you ask what motivates volunteers, you'll always hear,

"I love kids and want to serve Jesus." Good—but that's seldom *all* of what motivates a volunteer. Motivation is complicated; there's usually something else in there too.

Interviews give you the chance to dig a little deeper and develop a deeper understanding about what brought a volunteer to you—and what will help make that volunteer stick.

5. Interviews help you refer volunteers.

If you apply for a job at a big company in your town, you don't walk into the building and meet with the hiring supervisor right off the bat. The people in human resources will interview you first. They want to protect the hiring supervisor's time by only sending qualified candidates up for a personal interview.

I want to do the same thing for the volunteer supervisors at my church. I want to send the preschool supervisor only people who I think will fit in and who want to work in that area.

Interviewing volunteers is how you can make good referrals.

But the top reason you need to do interviews with every potential volunteer is...

6. Interviews get the right people into the right jobs.

Your goal is to get the right person into the right job at the right time for the right reasons. Interviews are *the* primary way to accomplish that.

At the interview you find out if a volunteer is spiritually mature and has time to do the job. You find out what's motivating the volunteer. You get a sense of whether a volunteer will get along with a specific supervisor.

That's a *lot* of information! And unless you interview people, you'll never collect it in a systematic, thorough way.

Is it really worth the effort? It is if you want to place a volunteer in a job and have that volunteer thrive. Without the information that comes from an interview, you're just guessing when it's time to make a placement.

People who do interviews remind me of those gardeners who have green thumbs. You know them—they're the people on your street who have flower pots on their porches and the plants are actually *alive*. Me, I can kill a cactus just by looking at it. When a mama plant wants to threaten her seedlings, she tells them if they aren't in bed in five minutes she's sending them to *my* yard.

I used to think people who could keep plants alive and move them from place to place were special somehow. They had a magic touch. But now I know that's not the case. They do have something I don't have, but it's not magic.

It's *information*.

Green thumb people take time to find out what sort of soil each plant likes. They pay attention so they transplant geraniums at the opportune moment, not the day after the first freeze. They nurture plants along and know the difference between a dahlia, a daisy, and a day lily.

As a result, their plants grow. Their flowers bloom. Scrawny little green twigs become tall, strong trees. And best of all, one plant can produce seeds that eventually fill up a garden with bright, vibrant color.

If you want your volunteers to thrive, you've got to know the difference between Harry, Henrietta, and Harvey. They don't all do well in the same soil. They need different amounts of sunshine and shade. They won't survive if you dump the same amount of water on them, tell them to have a good day, and never look at them again.

As for me, I want volunteers who thrive—and not just because they're the volunteers who do great ministry and make a children's ministry wonderful for kids. I want to see volunteers thrive because that's my ministry to *them*—to the volunteers themselves.

So don't rush into interviewing and do a poor job of it. That's not ministry to your volunteers. If you ask the wrong questions or do nothing with information you collect, you'll discourage people who want to serve. You'll actually chase volunteers *away*.

Here's what needs to happen before you start interviewing...

Select an Interviewing Approach

The big question: Will you centralize your church's volunteer interviewing or do it by departments?

Some churches set up a separate department to recruit and manage volunteers. The department's entire focus is connecting church members and volunteer roles.

There are a lot of reasons to recommend this approach, especially if your church has had a low participation in volunteering. You'll need people who can help church members discover how to use their abilities, skills, gifts, and passions for ministry.

In most churches, interviewing is a departmental thing—the children's pastor scouts for new volunteers, as does the youth pastor and every other ministry area leader. This free-for-all can lead to some problems...

Departmental interviewers only know about their own departments.
If your children's ministry recruiter decides not to use a potential volunteer, what then? Does that recruiter know where else to refer the potential volunteer?

There's competition among church departments.
I've been in churches where departments competed for resources, and I'll tell you this: I don't want to live like that again. It's no fun. It's destructive. I'd much rather we cooperate and trust that if God sends six great volunteers to the youth department, he'll send the next six to work with children.

Don't let departmental recruiters stalk around the church lobby, seeking whom they may devour.

Ministry areas grow lopsided.
This happens when you've got an outgoing, engaging department recruiter over in the usher ministry and a dry-as-bones recruiter staffing the youth department. Pretty soon you've got enough ushers to handle an NFL game and your youth ministry team disappears.

Centralizing the volunteer interviewing process fixes those problems. The folks doing the interviewing know about all the volunteer jobs in the church, and they're not pushing any particular department. But there's another alternative, and it's the one we use at my church.

We still recruit by departments, but our departments intentionally work together. We send people to one another. And we build in checks and balances so a department's need for a volunteer never becomes more important than placing that volunteer in the best possible spot.

I'll tell you more later about the approach we use at my church.

GET YOUR INTERVIEWERS READY

If you're in a small church, maybe you can do all the interviewing yourself. But if God grows your church, what then? I suggest you build the structure you'd use if you were a church five times your current size. That way when you do grow, you're all set. You're ready to receive God's blessing.

If you use volunteers as interviewers, handpick the people you want. This is one job where you must have people with developed skills and proven discernment. I've dropped in a job description for that volunteer role (see page 132).

Decide where you'll refer problems.

Let's say while Nancy is interviewing Denise, Denise starts talking to someone who's not there. Denise smiles and says that Abbadabba, the Atlantian warrior she channels, thinks Denise should work in junior church.

Hoo, boy.

Nancy already knows everything she needs to know about placing Denise in junior church: *It ain't gonna happen.* But Denise clearly needs help, and it's outside Nancy's depth. Where will Nancy send her?

Your interviewers must be able to make a referral to competent pastoral help. If that's your church's counseling ministry, fine. If it's your pastor, that's great. But decide *now* who'll be on the receiving end of referrals.

Let me say this again, in the clearest possible terms: Your interviewers shouldn't do pastoral counseling unless they're qualified pastoral counselors. Your volunteers are to help possible volunteers discern where God might best use them and their gifts in service. That's all.

You *must* set up a referral system—and teach your volunteers to use it.

children's ministry volunteers that stick

Determine where you'll keep information.

You're asking for personal information, so have a safe place to keep it. It can be in a locked cabinet or a password-protected file on the church computer, but make it secure. Since you're running background screening on applicants, you may be *required* by law to take measures to keep information confidential.

Back up your data. Don't let a computer crash in your church office destroy all your volunteer information.

While you're at it, enter basic information into a spreadsheet so you can track who's volunteering, where they're serving, and how long they've been on board. You'll need that information to design a recognition program for your volunteers.

Identify a place to do interviews.

You don't necessarily need an office for this. Anywhere you can talk without being overheard will work. Get to know the names of the counter staff at your local coffee house, and do your interviews there. Or meet with people in their homes. Just be sure you're never in a compromising situation.

Create a standard interview form.

You want interviewers to collect the same basic information from each potential volunteer. Some of it you'll need to run background checks and some to figure out where a volunteer might best serve.

Decide what you absolutely must know and create a form. You'll make the lives of your interviewers easier.

Here are two questions that you should always include...

- ***How did you become a Christian?*** How someone answers that tells you volumes. Explore a potential volunteer's spiritual journey.
- ***How busy are you these days?*** This open-ended question gets at how available someone is to do ministry. It explores the volunteer's life situation.

A potential volunteer may be a single parent working two jobs and raising three children. Or caring for an ailing parent. Or earning a college degree at night after a full day in the office. Each person has a different list of commitments, and those commitments have a *huge* impact on what volunteer role that person can fill.

Listen, if a volunteer can't follow through on a volunteer commitment, I don't want that person signing up for a job. He or she will feel guilty about not showing up, and I won't be happy, either.

If someone is willing but unable to volunteer, make a note so you follow up later. Someday that volunteer will finish that college degree, and you'll be there with a congratulations card and an invitation to use that degree as a volunteer at church. There isn't a college major you can't use if you give it enough thought.

Got your ducks lined up? Good.

Now let me tell you about the interview process we use at our church. It's not the only system you could choose, but it has served us well.

Our Interview and Placement Process

We recruit by departments. I've deputized my current children's ministry volunteers to recruit, so I'm not the only person looking for new staff. But no matter who makes contact with a potential volunteer, all roads lead to the Children's Ministry Volunteer Application.

It's the first of seven steps in our recruitment and placement process.

Step 1: The Children's Ministry Volunteer Application

Our volunteer application is four pages long and it gets personal. We ask for references. We expect applicants to give us permission to do background screening. It's a serious document.

My situation is unusual, because most people who volunteer for our children's ministry already know all about us. They're grateful parents who want to support the program that helped lead their children to Christ. Or they're people who were once *in* the program as children. I've got 150 volunteers who were once kids in our ministry and now they've come back to serve.

All of which means I don't normally need to help folks decide where they want to volunteer in our church. They want to serve in the Christian education department. The only question is where to plug them in.

Our volunteer application is pretty much our first interview. It gives us everything we need to know to do an initial screening and to be ready for a second, in-person interview.

I review every volunteer application personally. I could delegate that job, but I see reading applications as part of guarding the flock of children God has placed in my care. I look for anything that jumps out as not quite right. I make sure that my team has checked references and that a background screening has been completed. I read the results of those inquiries too.

I want to see if a volunteer's experience suggests a logical place for that person. If Samantha has a ton of preschool experience, I'll steer her toward our preschool department unless she indicates she wants to serve elsewhere.

If I'm satisfied, I make a few notes on the application and then initial it. Until I've OK'd the application, we don't move on to the next step—the in-person interview.

Step 2: The In-Person Interview

Volunteer interviews are conducted by paid staff members at my church—but they don't do the interviews alone.

If we expect Samantha will serve in the preschool area, the preschool supervisor sits in. We want that supervisor to have a say about whether Samantha is offered a volunteer job in the preschool.

Here's what's already lying on the desk when Samantha walks into the room: her completed application, her completed background screening, a copy of the code of conduct, and completed reference checks. There's no sense having the interview until that information is gathered.

The interview is mostly a discussion about what's on those sheets of paper. I want to make sure what's written on the application accurately reflects Samantha's heart. I want to go over our basic expectations of volunteers with Samantha to be sure she's in agreement. And we'll talk about any red flags that may have popped up on the paperwork.

If Samantha's been at six churches in the past ten years, we'll talk about that. If she got caught smoking dope when she was eighteen and that was fifteen years ago, I'll want to know what her behavior is like now. I'll ask if she's following the law now. And it will matter if she told us upfront that an arrest was going to show up on her background check.

You see, not every past criminal act will keep you from serving in our children's ministry. There's grace for some past mistakes—but it will certainly determine where we place you. If you got arrested for embezzling fifteen years ago, guess who's never going to count the offering?

Step 3: The Offer...or Not

At the end of the interview, we may wholeheartedly recommend Samantha for service. If so, we find out when she can begin. I always like for the supervisor to deliver the good news—it gets that relationship off to a great start.

If the supervisor doesn't want to "hire" Samantha, I tell Samantha we'll get back to her within a few days. I don't want to keep her hanging, but I also don't want to put her in a job where she's not wanted. The supervisor and I will talk after Samantha leaves to determine what either—or both—of us saw as a caution.

But whether she's accepted for service or put on hold until issues get resolved, no volunteer starts until I sign off on the paperwork. You see, I'm a big believer in checks and balances. My looking over the paperwork one last time is a final chance to see if anything jumps out at me. Is this the right person who's being put in the right job at the right time for the right reasons? It never hurts to ask that question one more time.

Step 4: Following Up After the Interview

After Samantha is placed in the preschool area, I want to know that the placement "took" and everyone is happy. So we check with Samantha and her supervisor separately after a few weeks. Is Samantha settling in? Any questions that haven't been answered? Any resources needed? Is everything going smoothly?

Step 5: Following Up Again in Two Months

Two months is plenty long enough for the shine to wear off a volunteer job. If there are problems that didn't come up during the interview and didn't surface the first few weeks of service, they're obvious by now.

My preschool pastor connects with Samantha and sees if she's received enough training to feel comfortable. Is the job working out? I ask for an update from the preschool pastor as well.

Step 6: Following Up One Month Before the End of the Term of Service

Let's say Samantha signed on for a six-month tour of duty in the preschool. That doesn't mean she *has* to leave in six months; it's the minimum stay. I hope she stays longer. I want Samantha to stick as a volunteer—in the preschool or elsewhere—for *decades*.

So we re-recruit Samantha while she's still on active duty. The preschool pastor visits her in the preschool classroom. We ask her how it feels to get hugs from the kids, to know she's helping them learn to love Jesus. We let her know she is an important part of our team and that she's appreciated. We ask what she's enjoyed about her volunteer job.

We help Samantha recognize the rewards of her volunteer service. Sure there have been dozens of spilled snacks. Sure there have been frazzled moms who forgot to say "thank you." That stuff happens. But what's gone right? How has she been fulfilled and had fun serving in the preschool? We ask her to share a couple of those stories with us—so we can share them with others.

The primary responsibility for retaining Samantha lies with her supervisor. But in our volunteers' eyes, those of us on the children's ministry staff are the Big Cheeses, the Head Freds—and a word or two from us counts, big time. That's true for you, too. Don't be too busy to re-recruit and reconnect your volunteers. You weren't too busy to help place them in your ministry; don't be too busy to say "thank you," too.

Step 7: Celebrate Longevity in Service

I recently got to hand out more than a hundred plaques to volunteers who've been with us for ten years or more. Those were volunteers who stuck!

But you're thinking, "What's this got to do with interviewing and placement? Handing out plaques is volunteer recognition!"

Yes and no. You won't have the opportunity to hand out plaques if you don't do careful interviewing and placement. You won't get the right people in the right jobs at the right time for the right reasons. You do that, and you'll have the joy of recognizing volunteers who've made a regular career of service.

And if that's not enough to motivate you, I don't know what is.

What If You Make a Mistake and Place a Volunteer in the Wrong Job?

Sometimes volunteers don't thrive where you—and they—thought they'd bloom. Even after all their best efforts, the volunteers are miserable, their supervisors are unhappy, and kids in their care aren't getting great ministry.

So move the volunteers elsewhere. There's no shame in trying something, finding it doesn't work, and then trying something else. That's how careers work sometimes.

Of course, it's one thing if the volunteer comes to us and says, "I thought I'd like working with junior highers and I've tried my best, but I just don't fit."

It's *another* thing if the volunteer thinks things are going fine, but it's obvious to everyone else she has no business in a preschool class. That's a more difficult situation.

So what do you do? You move her. You've got to. You don't have the right person in the right place at the right time for the right reasons. Somewhere, that's broken down and ministry to kids is suffering.

More than once I've gone to a volunteer and said, "I need to move you to another place of service where you can excel, where your gifts will help you."

Did the volunteers get offended? Sometimes they did. But usually they already knew there was a problem. If their supervisors were faithful in providing evaluations, issues were already on the table. And if the volunteers knew me and trusted that I wanted to help them succeed, they received my concern and transferred with no problem.

If you have to move a volunteer, that's a good time to evaluate what went wrong. I'm a *big* believer in pausing after you fix a problem to figure out how to never see that problem again.

Here's the honest truth: If you need to move a volunteer, the problem may not be with the volunteer. The problem may be with your interview system. Or with your job descriptions. Or with your supervisors. You won't know unless you take a close look and you ask some hard questions...

- *Does the job description adequately describe the needed skills and the scope of the work?* Ask the volunteer if he or she got blindsided by job expectations that weren't clear upfront. If so, revise the job description so it's accurate.
- *Has the supervisor provided coaching and training?* When volunteers fail, it can be a reflection on leadership. Look at the supervisor closely. Has this happened before? Do you see a trend? If so, train, or move, the supervisor.
- *Was it a bad fit from the start?* Did the volunteer feel "pushed" into this job by the interviewer? If so, train, or move, the interviewer.
- *Did the volunteer misrepresent his or her interests, skills, and availability?* Is the volunteer unwilling to do the work? Was the job too much for the volunteer for some reason? If so, be sure to place the volunteer in a more appropriate job to accommodate his or her limitations and schedule.

You've got volunteers plugged into jobs—good for you! You've got the right people in the right place. That's a great beginning.

Huh? Beginning? We're more than halfway through the book and it's just the *beginning*?

That's right, friend. You've got people doing ministry and that makes them volunteers. But those volunteers aren't yet volunteers who'll *stick*. You can still do things to influence that outcome and take them to the next level where they'll settle in for the long haul.

Ready for the next step? It's providing orientation, training, and evaluation.

chapter 8

Orientation, Training, and Evaluation

Volunteers who do their jobs well tend to be happier—
and stick longer. Here are three things you can do to
help them be spectacularly successful.

Once you've got the right volunteers in the right jobs, there are three things you can do right away to make these people successful in their jobs:

1. Get your volunteers oriented,
2. Get them trained, and
3. Evaluate their work.

Maybe those steps seem obvious to you, but they're *not* obvious to lots of churches. I can't tell you how many times I've gotten a blank stare when I asked if there was an orientation program for children's ministry volunteers at a church.

Buddy, it's important. Here's why...

VOLUNTEER ORIENTATION

When you start at a secular job, there's usually an orientation. It's the meeting where you fill out forms, find out about policies and procedures, and get a tour of the facility. You're told where to park, how to find the bathroom, and where your desk or locker is located.

An orientation reduces anxiety and gives you general

information about the organization. It gets you ready for the next day when you show up at your desk and begin training about your specific job.

Volunteers need orientations, too. Even if your volunteers came up through your Christian education department, there's information they need now that they didn't need then. And the classroom looks different when you're the teacher instead of a student.

ORIENTATION IS *NOT* YOUR ENTIRE TRAINING PROGRAM.

The first time I was introduced to the staff at the church where I serve, everyone was sitting in a big circle. I knew the pastor's name, and a few other people, but when folks zipped around that circle telling me their names and titles, it was a lost cause. There was *way* too much information coming at me.

For weeks I kept asking people to remind me of their names. I'm sure one or two people wondered why the pastor had hired a guy who couldn't even remember a name. The reason was simple: *information overload*.

When you try to cram everything a volunteer needs to know into one session, you're wasting your time. The volunteer can't retain it all. It's like trying to fill a water glass from a fire hose— there's too much coming at you for you to catch much.

So do this: Schedule a formal orientation program and design a training program to follow up the orientation. Each program has its own purpose.

THE FORMAL ORIENTATION

At this meeting all the new volunteers receive the same general information. An orientation meeting is a timesaver for ministry leaders and an encouragement to the volunteers. They need to see that they're not in this children's ministry thing alone.

Keep in mind that whatever you say verbally should also be on a handout or in your volunteer staff handbook. Information overload will erase most of what you say.

Here's what you need to cover at your formal orientation meeting:

Your ministry's vision statement and mission statement

Remind volunteers how their jobs connect to the ministry's larger vision and purpose. Talk about your mission statement and vision at every opportunity—and this is a prime chance!

The history of your church and children's ministry

Don't assume every volunteer knows this stuff. Provide a quick overview, emphasizing how your church fits into the community around you.

If your program has a history of drawing in unchurched kids, that's good for volunteers to know. If you're intentionally a resource for children with special needs, that's good to know too.

Basic logistics

When should volunteers be at their stations? How do you report attendance? Do you take an offering? What if you need a glue stick? Walk people around the Christian education area so they're familiar with the facility, too—especially where to find the janitor's closet.

And share the truly *important* information: where you keep the coffee pot.

The organizational chart

Walk volunteers through the organizational chart so they know who's around to serve them. Point out not only their supervisor, but also their supervisor's supervisor. Help volunteers see where they fit into the big scope of things.

Safety information

What happens if there's a severe storm? If the fire alarm goes off and kids have to be evacuated? If a tornado comes through? Cover the big stuff, but don't forget the little stuff, too. Show people where the first-aid kit is located, and have them practice filling out the incident report form they'll use if a child is hurt.

Communication

Will your volunteers receive a monthly e-mail or newsletter? Do you have a telephone tree? Can anyone go straight to the pastor with a suggestion, or do you prefer that volunteers work through you? Do you want to be called at home, or at the office, or both?

Cover all the basics. Let folks know how they can expect to receive information and how they should communicate with you.

Performance expectations

Run through the process by which people will be evaluated. Let folks know that everyone—you included—gets evaluated, and why. It's because you want to get better at what you do. And you'll help volunteers get better, too.

Handling of money

If a teacher needs something for her class, is she allowed to buy it and give the receipt to you for reimbursement? Is there a requisition procedure to follow to have a room painted? Is there a general budget for each classroom? What if a puppeteer needs a couple of new puppets?

Nothing sours a volunteer experience like being unsure of what to do about money. Cover this in a general sense. Explain your policies.

Distribution and review of orientation handbooks

I'm about to tell you to hand out your volunteer staff handbooks. And you're about to tell me that you don't have any, right? Well, we'll fix that. Your ministry needs policies and procedures, and your volunteers should know what they are.

Job descriptions tell volunteers what to do, but policies and procedures tell them how you want them to go about their jobs. On pages 143-144 I'll tell you what you should include in your handbook. Or you can order a copy of my church's handbooks. Call 1-800-888-7856 or visit our Web site at www.kidsonthe move.com. Don't skip this step—for several reasons:

A handbook fixes information overload.

It's a review of what you cover in the orientation, and it's available 24/7. Volunteers can get many of their questions answered without picking up the phone or stopping you in the hall.

A handbook forces you to make policy decisions now—while you're calm.

A policy is just a decision about how things should normally go. And the best possible time to determine that is while you're not under pressure.

Decide now how to handle situations your volunteers are likely to encounter. There are no angry parents glaring at you or screaming children demanding attention. It'll never be easier than right now to figure out what's usually the right thing to do and to describe that course of action.

A handbook reassures everyone in your ministry.

Flying by the seat of your pants may sound exciting, but when I walk by an open cockpit door as I file onto a 747 it's reassuring to see the pilots working their way through a preflight checklist. They aren't depending on their memories. They aren't figuring they'll make things up as they go.

A handbook sets expectations for your volunteers.

If you have behavior standards about appearance or church attendance, state those expectations in your handbook. Otherwise, how do you expect to hold volunteers accountable to those standards?

Questions and answers

There probably will be questions. There *should* be. Encourage and answer general questions that are of interest to all the volunteers present. If there are questions related to specific jobs, talk with the volunteer after the meeting.

Close with prayer

Don't just tell your volunteers you'll pray for them—*pray for them*. Right on the spot. In front of them.

Your formal orientation shouldn't take more than an hour, and *do* serve snacks. It's the first rule of working with volunteers: If you feed them, they will come.

Make the meeting as warm, friendly, and reassuring as possible. Remind volunteers that you won't toss them into deep water until they've learned to swim.

Which leads to the second part of getting volunteers settled into and successful in their jobs: training.

VOLUNTEER TRAINING

We Christians confuse "talking" with "training." We tell people what they should do, and think that's enough...but it's not.

You can't explain to a volunteer how to work with kids and expect that volunteer to be able to do it. That's like telling someone about pole vaulting and thinking they'll be able to go out and do it.

Now, I'm not a pole-vaulter. I'm not made for flight, if you get my drift. The only way I'd clear a pole hanging fifteen feet in the air (world-class pole-vaulters go even higher than *that*) is if you shot me out of a cannon.

But I've seen pictures of people pole-vaulting, and it doesn't look all that hard. You pick up a big stick, run toward the pole, shove the stick in a hole, and then sort of spring up over the pole. Assuming you remembered to put a mat on the other side so there's a soft landing, it doesn't seem too tough. I can explain it to you in about thirty seconds.

But that doesn't mean I can *do* it.

Looks can be deceiving, can't they? People who make things look easy usually do that because they've trained hard to master a skill. They've prepared and practiced until something hard comes naturally.

That's what I want for my children's ministry volunteers. I want them to be so prepared that when a discipline issue arises, they don't have to stop and think about what to do. They *know* what to do. It's automatic, because they're trained.

I want that for my volunteers because it means kids will have a great adult leader, but there's another reason, too: When someone is good at something, they tend to stick with it.

It's a fact of life: *It's harder to quit something you do well.*

Ever learn to play tennis? Your first lesson, you're awful. Every serve goes straight into the net. You can't hit the ball back.

If you *do* hit the ball, it sails over the fence and you've got to go fetch it.

You're doing tennis, but you aren't playing it.

Then something happens. One day you think, *I'm gonna smack this ball and drop it a foot from the base line*—and it happens! Just like you imagined it! You actually make a shot! Then, later in the set, you slam back another shot just the way you imagined it.

After that, tennis isn't all determination and pain. It gets to be fun...and you start to look forward to your lessons. That's because you've developed some skill, and you're starting to think of yourself as a tennis player.

You're hooked, friend. Tennis now owns you.

I want the same thing to happen with my volunteers. I want them to learn how to be so effective in working with children that they think of themselves as children's workers. When somebody at the office asks what they did over the weekend, I want my folks to say, "Well, we went to a movie, but the most fun thing I did was help fifteen third-graders learn about Jesus."

PEOPLE DON'T GET GOOD AT CHILDREN'S MINISTRY BY ACCIDENT.

If you want an excellent children's ministry, give your volunteer staff excellent training. There's no shortcut. And you've got to *continually* provide training, not try to do it all at once in an orientation or a class.

When you finish your orientation meeting or class, there's still stuff your volunteers need to know. But they don't know *what* they need to know.

I call it the "big dog factor."

Back when I was a paperboy, on every route there was at least one big dog. A big, *mean* dog. The kind of dog the owner kept fed because if it ever got hungry that owner was going to be lunch.

Now remember, this is back before the law required people with nasty dogs to put up warning signs. And this was the South, where nobody was about to let the government tell them they had to put their dogs on leashes. People with big, mean dogs let them lie around in the yard, in case the Yankees came back.

We paperboys learned quickly where the big dogs lived. We had to pedal our bikes fast past those houses and hang on the far side of the street. We'd whip a paper at those houses and if we hit the yard, that was good enough.

There was an orientation meeting for new paperboys, but I don't think any boy ever raised his hand and asked, "What about those big dogs? Where do the big, mean dogs live?"

Did new paperboys need that information? They sure did. But they didn't *know* they needed it—not until they were lolly-gagging down the street and a hundred pounds of teeth and bad attitude exploded out of a yard and tore off after them.

At your orientation meeting, your volunteers are like those paperboys: *They don't yet know what they need to know.* They won't figure that out until they're in the job for a few weeks. *That's* when they'll have questions for you.

And you've got to be there for them.

To really do training, I think you need to give every one of your volunteers a coach. In our church we call coaches "master teachers," and it's their job to teach people under them three things:

- how to perform their jobs,
- what they're not supposed to do in their jobs, and
- what to do if something unusual happens.

Isn't that what you want from your volunteers? For them to know what to do, what not to do, and what to do when something throws a curveball at them? That's my definition of a perfectly trained volunteer.

THE MASTER TEACHER SYSTEM

We use the master teacher system every place we can, but you see it at its best in our classrooms.

If you're a new classroom teacher, you'll be teamed up with a master teacher who has lots of experience and a desire to come alongside you and help you learn the ropes. Here's how you'll be trained:

First, you'll watch. The first few weeks you'll watch the master teacher in action. You'll see what she does and debrief with her. She'll explain what she's doing and why.

Second, you'll lead a few activities. Once you've been in the classroom for a couple of months, you'll try leading some classroom activities. The master teacher will let you run with them—but when the class ends, you'll be evaluated so you know where you were strong and where you need some help.

Third, you'll lead a full lesson. When you're ready, you'll lead a lesson from start to finish. The master teacher will give you feedback designed to help you improve. Our volunteers don't resent input from master teachers; they value it. Expert advice helps teachers serve the children more effectively.

Finally, you'll be evaluated regularly. No one ever graduates from being evaluated. It's a constant thing; master teachers, coordinators, even my other children's pastors are evaluated frequently so they know how they're doing.

That's a training program: individual attention, constant coaching, and an opportunity to learn skills gradually.

That's not to say that other kinds of training aren't needed too. They are. Here are some of the training opportunities we make available for our volunteers:

MAGAZINES AND OTHER EDUCATION MATERIALS

Make it a habit to pass around articles, books, and anything else that gets your volunteers thinking. Encourage volunteers to read articles and ask, "How can we apply that lesson here in our corner of the world?"

I make my interns read through a short list of books so we can talk about issues raised in the books. I loan them my personal copies so I find out how long it took them to read the books and so they know I'm serious.

I've got a column in Children's Ministry Magazine that's just been a dream come true, and I'm all the time giving my staff copies of the material I send to the magazine. I hand it over and say, "Here, y'all. Read this. This guy's *good.*"

So far nobody's had the courage to disagree with me, but if they did—if they came back and said, "Brother Jim, I just can't agree with this at all"—well, we'd have something to discuss, wouldn't we? If I'm going to help my volunteers grow, I've got to know what they're thinking.

CLASSES AND SEMINARS

They don't all cost a fortune. Some are dirt-cheap—you can send your whole team to a half-day seminar for the cost of sending one person to a full-blown conference in another city.

If you buy curriculum, call your local Christian bookstore or the publisher's sales rep and ask if they've got anyone who can stop by to show your folks how to use it most effectively.

If you live near a Christian college that has a Christian education program, find out what they're doing. How about if you host a class at your church building? What would it cost to have a professor do a workshop?

And don't ignore what people learn at work. Encourage your children's workers to be constant learners, always thinking, "How can I use this in my ministry?"

STAFF MEETINGS

All the time I hear, "Brother Jim, I just can't get volunteers to come out to staff meetings. They just won't show up, the lazy people."

May I ask you a question? Are your staff meetings worth attending?

People will generally make time for what they think is important. If your meetings help volunteers be better at their jobs and help them be better parents and believers, they'll show up.

Now, I doubt you deliberately set out to help your children's ministry volunteers be better parents, but that's what happens. If Francine learns to be more patient with other people's kids, she'll be more patient with her own.

Don't hold a staff meeting if you don't have anything to say. You can write down information and e-mail it to volunteers. If you're going to meet, do something that develops volunteers' skills and requires that they attend for them to benefit.

Respect volunteers' time—and your own time, too.

Tapes, CDs, and videos

It's not *just* because I have a monthly leadership resource ministry that I'm all for having tapes and CDs for your volunteers. It's also because I know how busy people are. (By the way, check out the Children's Ministers Leadership Club at www.jimwideman.com.)

Some folks can't come to training meetings. We've got pilots who volunteer at our church—they never know their schedules from month to month. We've got nurses, doctors, and others who work odd shifts. They can cover their volunteer roles, but after that it's hit and miss, and there's not much that can be done about it.

So I give them tapes and CDs to listen to in the car as they're driving to work. Or maybe they listen in while they're working out or walking. I don't care what they're doing so long as they soak in the information I want them to have.

Peer mentoring

This is for you: Go find a couple churches about the size of your church, and get whoever is in charge of children's ministry at those places to meet you for coffee. Agree to all bring your volunteer staff handbooks, your registration sheets, and whatever else you use to stay organized, and compare notes.

And when you *really* get to trust one another, bring along a copy of your children's ministry budgets to compare. How do other churches use their money? Why do they spend it like they do? You'll learn a *lot*.

A group like this will help you in so many ways. For instance, you may find that the best training you can give your nursery supervisor is to ask her to observe in another church's nursery for a few weeks, to see what they do. Then ask her to bring back the best ideas she saw. Another church may want to send a team over to your place to see how you decorated a basement so it wasn't depressing for your kids.

Why Churches Don't Do Enough Training

Most churches *say* the key to having a great children's ministry is to have excellent training and supplies—but then those resources aren't provided because of the expense.

I'm all for saving a buck. I can't remember the last time I paid retail for a ministry resource. Sam's Club is about ready to give me my own parking spot, I buy so much stuff from them for our Sunday school.

I've pointed out some ways you can get inexpensive—or free—training, but sooner or later you're going to want to shake the money tree and have enough fall out to get you or a staff member to a conference.

Let me suggest a way I've found to get your board to part with enough money to make that training conference happen. It's a three-step campaign.

1. Connect with your pastor and church board on a regular basis.

Here's a mistake many children's ministry leaders make: They ignore their pastors. They don't keep church leadership posted about what they're doing and how it's going. Big mistake.

You don't want the first time you meet your pastor to be the day you're showing up in the pastor's office with your hat in your hand, asking for a bump up in the budget. That's a bad first impression, bud.

Show what you're doing with what you've got when it comes to training resources. If you've found that the local chamber of commerce hosts an "effective communication" class, and you've enrolled three of your adult class teachers in it for $10 each, let your pastor know. Demonstrate that you're a good steward of what you've got, and you'll be given more.

2. Connect the training with your vision statement and mission statement.

Your church board and pastor have already endorsed your children's ministry vision and mission. So make a strong case to show that the training you seek will help move your ministry toward fulfilling that vision and mission.

Pick your training conference carefully. Explain how it will network you with relevant mentors and let you gather useful information.

3. Connect training with results.

Which do you think is more compelling: "I want to go to a conference" or "I want to attend the Children's Ministry Seminar because there are six sessions I've identified that will help me recruit and train the folks we'll need when we add that second service next year"?

The second one is the one that'll win your pastor's heart.

Why? Because it shows you've thought about the results you want to see as a result of the training. And because the results you want to see support your pastor's vision for growing the church.

When it comes to budget, you're not going to get everything you want. I know, because after twenty-five years in children's ministry, I've never gotten everything *I* wanted...and I don't ask for the moon.

Do this: Show your pastor how you're saving training money everywhere you can, and leave it up to God to convince whoever controls your church budget about whether you should get more money.

But now and then remind the people who control the purse strings: Ministries are only as good as their training and supplies.

Volunteer Evaluation

For most people, *evaluation* is an awful word. When they've been evaluated at work they heard their boss recite a list of things they'd done wrong.

That's not how evaluations work at our church—and if you want to have volunteers stick with you, it better not describe how evaluations go at your church either.

Train your ministry supervisors to *redefine* what it means to be evaluated. I say *train* because they've probably hated evaluations, too. The only way to do the training is for you to model what a positive, helpful evaluation looks like. Then, when you've finished evaluating the people who report to you, say, "I want you to do evaluations exactly the same way."

Here's what a helpful evaluation looks like:

It's frequent. If you see someone do something that needs correcting, don't wait for three months to tell him or her. Take that person aside and address the issue immediately.

It's private. Especially if there's something that's corrective, do it away from the public view. Praise in public, but correct in private.

It's specific. It's not helpful to say, "You should do a better job disciplining kids." What does that mean exactly? It's far more helpful to say, "When Johnny takes a hostage, you should call the SWAT team sooner." See the difference?

It's affirming. By far the majority of the feedback you give volunteers should be positive. I've heard it said that it takes nine positive comments to balance out one negative one, but I think that's low. Make it twenty to one.

So now your volunteers are interviewed...in place...motivated...relationally connected...oriented...trained...evaluated ...what's next? How can you turn your volunteers into long-term, happy-camper, last-forever volunteers?

What's the secret?

At last it's time to pull back the veil and reveal the *one thing* that makes all the difference. The *one thing* that turns volunteers who used to bail out at six months into volunteers that stick for years.

chapter 9

The Secret of Volunteers Who Stick

The secret revealed...and you'll never guess what it is.

So what's the secret? How do you get volunteers to stick longer than the minimum commitment you required when they joined your ministry?

It's easy: Keep doing what you've been doing. Execute the fundamentals you've just put into practice.

That's it.

Honest.

There's no silver bullet or magic pill or secret handshake.

If you've done the work I've suggested so far, the natural consequence will be that a greater and greater percentage of your volunteers will renew their commitment to volunteering in your church. That's what creating a volunteer-friendly culture will do for you.

And if you've written the job descriptions, done interviewing, and carefully placed people in volunteer jobs, more and more of your people will stick. They'll be having too good a time to leave.

It all sounds too simple, doesn't it? But believe me—executing the fundamentals with excellence pays off. It pays off in wonderful ministry now and in making recruitment easy later because volunteers want to stay.

Now, I knew you wouldn't believe me. That's why I asked some of my volunteers who stick to share what's kept them around for so long...

When Patty Daugherty thinks about her volunteer work at church, she doesn't just think about the children. "I've met some of my best friends in the preschool department," she says. "They're people I didn't know before, but I cherish them now."
Patty has been serving for nine years.

Charlotte Uzzel enjoys the same benefit from serving. "It's the most beautiful relationship," she says of her friends who are volunteers. "As we volunteers walk through life we look at each other and realize how much we have in common. We pray for each other often."
Charlotte is a master teacher who's served for seven years.

For Janet Harris, a twelve-year volunteer career at our church has taken some twists and turns. "When I came to Church On The Move, I'd been a music leader with adults, but not with kids. But that was my vision: I wanted to work with kids and music."
That's not where Janet landed at first. She was a greeter, then worked in the nursery. Then she served in a toddler room, then with the three-year-olds. "Every place I served was a chance to be faithful and to learn something," says Janet. "I always got something I could use later."
In addition to being one of our worship leaders, Janet is presently an assistant master teacher with our younger elementary children as well as my executive assistant.

Roger Diamond has worked with kids for years—as a children's pastor in a Texas church for a while. He's been with us for ten years and says he loves ministering to and loving kids. And he's allowed to do that in part because of how our ministry is organized.
"The job descriptions give everyone a clear idea of what they're doing," Roger says. "And we're not stuck in a corner by ourselves, unsure what to do. Supervisors stop by weekly and if there's something I need, I just say so."

Jeanne Diamond, Roger's wife, recently resigned after ten years as a children's ministry volunteer. "I wanted some time to be home, focused on my family," Jeanne says.

When she gave thirty days' notice to her supervisor, Jeanne says she felt no guilt or condemnation. "He said he trusted that I'd heard from the Lord, and he supported my taking time off. He asked God to bless me, and celebrated my service."

And what impact does that kind of supervisory understanding have on Jeanne? "I know the door is always open to come back and volunteer," she says, "and I expect that in time that's just what I'll do."

Glad to hear it, Jeanne. I've got your old application in a file on my desk, ready to reactivate. I can't wait. We're going to have a great time praising God and serving some kids.

There are other stories, too. Hundreds of them. Too many to recount here.

They're the right people in the right jobs at the right time for the right reasons. They've connected with our ministry's vision and mission and formed relationships that give them something precious in exchange for their volunteer efforts.

And it's all a natural outcome of doing the things you'll do in your ministry as you implement the steps outlined in this book.

You reap what you sow, and as you sow into the lives of volunteers the harvest is great—for your ministry and the kingdom of God.

God bless you.

Have fun.

Here are forms you can photocopy or adapt to your needs, handouts for your leaders, and outlines and templates for job descriptions, volunteer handbooks, and more.

job description template

Job title:

This position is supervised by:

The goal of this position:

Here's what the person in this job will do:
-
-
-
-
-

The time required per week/month to accomplish this job with excellence:

You are committing yourself to faithfully fulfill this job, unless the Lord directs you elsewhere, for a period of:

Training that will be provided to you includes:

Here are special qualifications or unique skills the position requires:

Job title: Volunteer Interviewer

This position is supervised by: Children's Pastor

The goal of this position: To assist potential volunteers in finding the most appropriate volunteer jobs within the Christian education department or in other ministry areas of the church.

Here's what the person in this job will do:
- Work through the Children's Ministry Volunteer Form with volunteer applicants.
- Initiate background screening on every volunteer applicant using the approved background screening procedure.
- Arrange follow-up interviews between screened volunteer applicants and Christian education ministry leaders.

The time required per week/month to accomplish this job with excellence: A half-day training seminar on interviewing and active listening and approximately five hours per week (two one-hour interviews, plus paperwork completion and follow-up phone calls).

You are committing yourself to faithfully fulfill this job for a period of: six months.

Training that will be provided to you includes: a half-day seminar, coaching sessions with the children's pastor as required or desired, and quarterly meetings with the Christian education ministry leaders.

Here are special qualifications or unique skills the position requires:
- You must be a skilled listener.
- You must be able to handle confidential information in an appropriate fashion.
- You must have been a volunteer in a ministry here at our church.
- You must maintain an awareness of the varied volunteer positions available in our church.

Job title: Master Teacher

This position is supervised by: Children's Pastor

The goal of this position: The master teacher assumes responsibility for monitoring and supervising all activities in his or her classroom.

Here's what the person in this job will do:
- Start and end class on time.
- Work with the children's pastor in making all monitor and supervisor assignments for the master teacher's class.
- Train volunteers assigned to the master teacher's classroom.
- Complete a master teacher checklist for each service, as well as make sure each volunteer in the master teacher's class knows his or her job duties.
- Assist the children's pastor in recruiting volunteers, making sure all new volunteers have been approved.

The time required per week/month to accomplish this job with excellence: Monthly master teacher meetings are required, as are quarterly Christian education department meetings. Each master teacher will be expected to direct a classroom three weeks per month and to be regularly attending adult worship opportunities at our church.

You are committing yourself to faithfully fulfill this job for a period of: six months.

Training that will be provided to you includes: monthly peer meetings, quarterly Christian education department meetings, and coaching sessions with the children's pastor as required or desired. Also, a one-day training event will be held each year.

Here are special qualifications or unique skills the position requires:
- You must have served as an assistant master teacher for at least one year.
- You must be teachable.
- You must have a good knowledge of the Bible.
- You must be faithful in church and past volunteering attendance.
- You must be in agreement with the teachings and policies of our church.
- You must have a servant's heart and be willing to do what it takes to get the job done.

Job title: Registration Desk Volunteer

This position is supervised by: Registration Desk Coordinator

The goal of this position: The registration desk volunteer makes sure the registration process for children's classrooms is organized and progresses smoothly.

Here's what the person in this job will do:
- Oversee and assist in the registration process for regular attendees, first-time visitors, and adult visitors.
- See that all forms and supplies are ready before children arrive for a service and are securely returned to the registration desk after the service.
- Complete a registration checklist for each service for which the registration supervisor is responsible.
- Communicate all needs, questions, and/or problems concerning registration to the registration desk coordinator.

The time required per week/month to accomplish this job with excellence: The registration desk volunteer meetings are required, as are quarterly Christian education department meetings. Each registration desk volunteer will be expected to serve three weeks per month and to be regularly attending adult worship opportunities at our church.

You are committing yourself to faithfully fulfill this job for a period of: six months.

Training that will be provided to you includes: monthly newsletter, quarterly Christian education department meetings, and coaching sessions with the registration desk coordinator as required or desired. Also, a one-day training event will be held each year.

Here are special qualifications or unique skills the position requires:
- You must be teachable.
- You must have a good knowledge of the registration policies and procedures.
- You must be familiar with the children's ministry wing.
- You must be faithful in attendance.
- You must be in agreement with the teachings and policies of our church.
- You must have a servant's heart and be willing to do what it takes to get the job done.

FOR CHILDREN'S MINISTRY

Confidentiality Information

This application is to be completed by all applicants for any position (volunteer or compensated) within our church. Its use helps the church provide a safe and secure environment for those who participate in our programs and use our facilities.

General Information

Date: _____

Name: _____

Address: _____

City: _____ State: _____ ZIP: _____

Phone: ( ) _____ E-mail _____

Male ❑ Female ❑   Birth date: _____ Marital status: _____

Number of children: _____

Spouse's name (if married): _____

Anniversary date (if married): _____

Is your spouse involved in a ministry at our church? ❑ yes ❑ no

If yes, in what role and what department: _____

Maiden name: _____

Your Social Security number: _____

Alias (or other names you've gone by): _____

Present employer: _____

May we call you at work? ❑ yes ❑ no   Work phone: ( ) _____

Christian Experience

Are you a member of our church? ❑ yes ❑ no

How long have you attended our church? _____

Do you tithe on a regular basis to our church? ❑ yes ❑ no

Have you ever completed a volunteer application at our church before?

❑ yes ❑ no

If yes, for what department? _____ When? _____

Do You Believe...

YES NO

❑   ❑   In the virgin birth and deity of Jesus Christ?

❑   ❑   That people receive forgiveness of sins and eternal life through
a relationship with Jesus?

(continued on page 136)

YES NO [Fill in the faith essentials for your church]

❑ ❑ _____

❑ ❑ _____

❑ ❑ _____

❑ ❑ _____

Christian Ministry Experience

List the names and addresses of other churches you've attended regularly during the past five years:

Church _____ Church _____

Address _____ Address _____

City, State _____ City, State _____

Pastor _____ Pastor _____

Reason for leaving _____ Reason for leaving _____

List any gifts, training, education, or other factors that have prepared you for Christian service: _____

_____

Describe your experiences sharing your faith with others:_____

_____

Have you ever been involved in children's ministries before? ❑ yes ❑ no

If yes, in what areas?_____

With what church or organization? _____

Why do you want to be involved in our children's ministry? _____

_____

Lifestyle Questions

Do you have any limitations or conditions preventing you from performing certain types of activities relating to children's ministry? ❑ yes ❑ no

If yes, please explain: _____

Have you been accused of and/or convicted of child abuse or a crime involving actual or attempted sexual molestation of a minor? ❑ yes ❑ no

If yes, please explain: _____

Desired Involvement

INDICATE AREAS OF INTEREST

Please indicate the areas of ministry in which you would like to serve, in order of preference (for example, 1,2,3...).

HUGS

❑ Hospitality
❑ Ushers
❑ Greeters
❑ Safety/Traffic

Youth Ministries

❑ Wednesday night service
❑ Bus Driver
❑ Weekend Junior High ministry

Music Ministries

❑ Musician
❑ Singer
❑ Computer/Displays/Lyrics

Children's Ministries

❑ Nursery
❑ Toddlers and twos
❑ Preschool
❑ Pre-K and Kindergarten
❑ Lower elementary
❑ Upper elementary

[Add other areas of involvement in your church such as care ministries, outreach ministries, Christian education ministries, support ministries, and recreation ministries, and list jobs in each area.]

Is your spouse and/or family in agreement with you working in our ministry?
❑ yes ❑ no
Which weekend service(s) do you normally attend? ❑ Saturday
❑ Sunday 9 a.m. ❑ Sunday 11 a.m.

Which service(s) are you able to work in? ❑ Saturday ❑ Sunday 9 a.m.
❑ Sunday 11 a.m. ❑ Wednesday ❑ Bus ministry

Personal References

(No employees or relatives. Please include at least one former senior pastor, associate pastor, or ministerial supervisor.)

Name —————————————— Name ——————————————

Address ————————————— Address ——————————————

City, State ———————————— City, State ——————————————

Phone ( ) —————————— Phone ( ) ——————————————

Name ——————————————

Address —————————————

City, State ————————————

Phone ( ) ——————————

Applicant Statement

The information contained in this application is correct to the best of my knowledge. I give the church permission to complete a background check on me. I authorize any references or churches listed in this application to give you any information they may have regarding my character and fitness for helps ministries. I release all such references from liability for any damage that may result from furnishing such evaluations to you, and I waive any right that I have to inspect the references provided on my behalf. Should my application be accepted, I agree to be bound by the constitution and bylaws and policies of [church] and to refrain from unscriptural conduct.

Applicant's Signature:————————————— Date:——————

Witness:——————————————————— Date:——————

For Office Use Only

❑ Approved for ministry

❑ Not approved for ministry

Date ————————————————————————

Comments ———————————————————————

a children's
ministry guide to

INTERVIEWING CHURCH VOLUNTEERS

God has placed you in an important place! You'll help church members find places to use their God-given abilities, skills, gifts, and passions for ministry here at our church. You're cooperating with God's purposes—and helping church members do the same.

You'll receive comprehensive training about how to use the interview form, but this brief introduction will get you started in preparing for your job as a volunteer interviewer.

YOUR PURPOSE

Your job is to gather information and to discern where a potential volunteer might fit in our church's ministries. You won't offer anyone a job—that's up to the supervisor in the ministry area you recommend.

But you *will* steer potential volunteers toward job placement, so it's important you approach your job prayerfully. Ask God for keen discernment, an open heart and mind, and an ability to listen well.

To accomplish your purpose, you need to be familiar with all the volunteer jobs in our church. You need to know where there are openings and where there are waiting lists. So regularly review all the job descriptions in our database, and stay current about which ministries are seeking staff members.

HOW TO CONDUCT AN INTERVIEW

Every person whom you interview is being interviewed by choice. You'll almost always find people open, honest, and cooperative.

But not always.

There are wolves out among the sheep, and we want to identify them before they prey on our flock. That's why you can never skip addressing any part of the interview form. You may also never, under any circumstances, skip getting permission to run a background check.

If a potential volunteer refuses to give permission for a background check, that person cannot serve in children's ministry. No exceptions. Point out that you've had a screening, as have all the other staff and pastors. It's a requirement for insurance purposes, and it's a requirement to be faithful protectors of our children.

Here are the basic steps of conducting an interview:

• THE PRE-INTERVIEW

Before you meet with a potential volunteer, review the interview form. Review the job descriptions, and check to see which jobs are open. Pray for guidance, wisdom, and discernment. Review what you know, if anything, about the person being interviewed. Check to be sure the place you've chosen to conduct the interview will still work—is it sufficiently private, free of distractions, and quiet enough for you to conduct a conversation?

And be sure to arrive ten minutes early so you can relax a bit. Interviews are often as stressful for interviewers as for people being interviewed.

• OPENING THE INTERVIEW

The first few minutes of your interview are critical. It's when you can put the potential volunteer at ease with a warm greeting and the offer of a cup of coffee or a soft drink.

Don't dive into the interview form itself; establish a rapport and put the potential volunteer at ease.

• THE INTERVIEW

Remind the potential volunteer why you're meeting: to help the person discern the best possible fit for volunteer service in the church. Point out that this interview isn't like a job interview, with the results being either getting the job or not getting it.

Explain the process we follow. You'll gather information and suggest a fit between the volunteer and a volunteer role. You'll then set up a meeting between the potential volunteer and the person who supervises the ministry area you're recommending. You'll take care of paperwork, and you'll arrange for a background screening.

That's right—mention the background screening right up front.

Give the potential volunteer every opportunity to tell you if something will appear on the report that will raise questions.

The interview form starts with general questions because those are the easiest to answer. As you fill in the blanks, establish a rapport with the potential volunteer. It will make asking the later questions easier.

When you ask questions, listen carefully. Make eye contact, ask follow-up questions to dig a little deeper, but don't interrupt their answers as volunteers share.

Invite questions from the person you're interviewing too. Potential volunteers are deciding if they really want to commit themselves to serving in a church ministry. They're checking us out, too. Tell them whatever you can.

• MAKING A PLACEMENT

If someone expresses a strong desire to serve in some specific part of children's ministry, we'll honor that if possible. Tell the person what jobs exist and if any of those positions are open. There's a waiting list for some of the jobs; ask if the person being interviewed would consider a different position for a period of time. If that's the case, indicate it on the interview form, and we'll contact the volunteer when a preferred job opens up in order to check interest at that point.

But we'll check back *only* if you indicate a preferred job on the form.

If you discern there's a strong match between the volunteer and a specific job, go through that job description in detail. Explain why you think it's a strong match. Ask if the potential volunteer would be willing to explore it in more detail. If the answer is "yes," promise to have the supervisor of that position call to arrange a follow-up meeting.

If the answer is "no," ask for an explanation. You may have misunderstood the potential volunteer's heart or not clearly understood his or her experience or call from God. Seek understanding.

A potential volunteer might not like any of the possible jobs you've presented. If that's the case, it's very likely the person doesn't belong in children's ministry. Explore jobs located in other departments. *It's better to place a volunteer somewhere than to place that person nowhere.* We want to serve our fellow departments, not compete with them!

When you've come up with a plan of action, put it in writing on the form. That way you'll both be clear about who will do what, and when.

If there's a follow-up meeting to arrange, you do the arranging. Don't let a potential volunteer walk out promising to call a ministry area leader. *You* make that call, and see that we keep the initiative on our end. Summarize what will happen next with potential volunteers before they leave.

And never leave an interview without thanking God in prayer for the meeting.

- **CLOSING IN PRAYER**

Thank God for what God is in the process of doing in the volunteer's life—and in the life of the children's ministry and the church.

Note to interviewer: What items caught your attention on the volunteer application? List them below for discussion:

-
-
-

What items caught your attention on the background screening? List them below for discussion:

-
-

What items caught your attention during the reference checking? List them below for discussion:

-
-
-

Questions to ask applicant:

How did you become a Christian?

How busy is your life these days?

In light of your past experience, your gifts, and your demonstrated skills, abilities, and passion for ministry, we want to suggest you serve in this role: _____
How do you feel about taking a volunteer role in that area?

Here are categories of policies and procedures I suggest you include in your handbook...

SAFETY PROCEDURES

The time to decide where to take kids when a tornado alarm sounds isn't when the alarm goes off. Think through evacuation plans, severe storm plans, the placement of first aid kits, and a notification system to use in case someone is hurt.

Also include standards about when and where adults can be with children. Even harmless situations can look questionable when a parent rounds the corner and sees a child alone with an adult. Use your policies to protect volunteers themselves from making poor decisions.

SECURITY PROCEDURES

However you check children in and out, be clear about it. If you have a lock-down policy, spell it out. Who is allowed where? when? why?

Also include a statement about background screenings. Who needs them? I'd suggest your policy be that anyone serving in children's ministry needs one. That policy makes everything thorough and removes any room for folks to say you're playing favorites.

FACILITY ISSUES

Is it OK to bring in your own classroom supplies? To move the projector from one room to another without reserving it? How do you go about making twenty-five copies of a handout sheet? Use the handbook to spell out clearly the rules about using the church's equipment.

APPEARANCE STANDARDS AND OTHER BEHAVIOR STANDARDS

I mentioned this earlier: If you have expectations of your volunteers, spell them out. If you care how people look when they're working with your kids, say so. If you have standards concerning tobacco, alcohol, or drug use, be clear about them. Make sure there are no surprises for your volunteers.

REGULARLY SCHEDULED MEETING ATTENDANCE

What happens if someone refuses to come to quarterly meetings? Well, nothing—if you haven't set a policy that participation is expected. It's up to you to make the meetings worthwhile, but it's your policy that makes them mandatory.

REGISTERING COMPLAINTS

If something goes wrong or there's suspected wrongdoing, what should a volunteer do?

Outline a procedure. Tell volunteers the name of the person to whom they should report their concerns, and if that person isn't receptive, whom else to notify. A policy like this opens up a clear channel for conflict resolution. Problems will be addressed before they reach hurricane-force status.

PERFORMANCE REVIEWS

When and how will volunteers be evaluated? Clearly outline the process so nobody is surprised. Be sure your policy communicates that the primary purpose of evaluations is to celebrate accomplishments and build skills.

ADVANCEMENT

How do you get promoted around your church? by seniority?

through demonstrating skills? Is a volunteer stuck in the same job forever? What if the volunteer wants to move up—or over into another area?

You'll improve the odds of volunteers sticking if you address this issue. People who are faithful in small things want the chance to be faithful in larger things.

Your church already has a policy about this, you know. It's however your church has operated in the past. That's your existing policy, even if it's never been written down. Is it how you want to operate in the future?

And here are some things that should most definitely not be in your volunteer staff handbook…

• Don't put in anything you don't intend to enforce.

• In the business world, employees have challenged handbook policies that *were* enforced (like drug testing) because there were other listed policies that *weren't* enforced (like giving two weeks' notice before vacations). In other words, if part of the handbook doesn't matter, the whole thing doesn't matter.

• You aren't a business, but the principle holds: Be serious about everything in your handbook. Don't train volunteers to think it's a *suggestion* book instead of a rule book.

• Don't include lists you have to update every two weeks. Instead, put this kind of information on handouts and update them when necessary.

DON'T ADD SPECIFICS

It's fine to say, "Lock all doors and windows when leaving the building." But don't say, "Lock all five exterior doors and check and lock all twenty-one exterior windows, paying special attention to the far north window in the third classroom on the west side of the education wing hallway, as it tends to stick."

GET SIGNATURES ON THE DOTTED LINE

When you give volunteers their handbooks, don't assume the handbooks will be read. Ask volunteers to sign a sheet that indicates they promise to read the handbooks. Keep that sheet in their information folders.

Policies and procedures that never get read are worthless, so force this issue.

AND FINALLY, KEEP YOUR POLICIES CURRENT

Revisit your policies every year so you stay current. I'm not suggesting you rewrite a policy just to rewrite it, but I am suggesting you review each policy and ask, "Is this the best way we can do this? Has our mission or culture changed in such a way that we should change this policy?"

Pay especially close attention to safety and security policies. The law and our culture are shifting quickly concerning how much parents trust the church. Our policies and procedures must be state-of-the-art if we're going to be perceived as trustworthy. We've got to go the second mile, and even the third and fourth miles.